A BRIEF EXI

ROMANS

A BRIEF EXPOSITION OF
ROMANS

The Abide Series

SCOTT GILCHRIST

Abiding
Media Press

A Brief Exposition of Romans

Abiding Media Press
14605 SW Weir Road
Beaverton, OR 97007

Edited by Mark Loomis

ISBN (paperback): 9781662923616
eISBN: 9781662923623

CONTENTS

FORWARD

Scott Gilchrist is an expositor's expositor! In 2001, not long after my wife and I had moved to Portland, Oregon, I heard about a pastor known for his verse-by-verse exposition of the Bible. I had to hear him, so one Sunday evening, I drove the 25 miles across the Willamette River from East Portland to Beaverton to Southwest Bible Church. Sitting in the back of the large auditorium, I opened my Bible to the book of Numbers and heard a 40-minute sermon that confirmed all the great things I had heard about him. After the service, I met Scott and began a friendship that would develop into a ministry partnership about ten years later.

The person who had told me about this Bible teacher was a retired SIM missionary and member of Southwest Bible Church, John Corey. Meeting him would likewise have a direct impact on the course of my ministry. John was the ultimate disciple and mentor of young pastors in Africa and Russia, even in his retirement years and even after he was diagnosed with multiple myeloma. He inspired me with his stories of leading men in the study of the Word, especially during short trips back to Liberia, where he had served as a missionary years before. Through his and Scott Gilchrist's invitation, I was offered the opportunity to lead and expand what had become known as the Romans Project (see the appendix for more information). For the next five years, it was my joy to travel throughout Africa and Southeast Asia promoting the repeated reading (20 times) and handwriting (one time) of Romans and then distributing to the thousands of pastors who did so, Mp3 players with Scott Gilchrist's teaching on numerous books of the Bible. At last count, around 20,000 pastors have completed the Romans Project requirements and received the Mp3 players.

Of all the positive comments I heard from pastors and church leaders who had received the Mp3 players, my two favorites were: "It is like having a Bible College in my pocket!" and "Pastor Scott Gilchrist has become my pastor." I think those comments summarize well what I find in this book. You will be blessed to read Scott's careful exposition of the text of Romans blended perfectly with the comments and illustrations of a seasoned pastor. He is clear and concise in explaining each section, even the more difficult ones. He occasionally uses his Greek knowledge to clarify meanings of keywords without overwhelming the reader with complicated exegetical verbiage. His illustrations flow from his experiences as a lifelong witness, sharing the gospel of Romans in real life with real impact in lives, not just as a pastor who teaches the gospel in Romans well.

I was privileged to hear Scott teach Romans in five days in Addis Ababa, Ethiopia, which became the teaching of Romans on the Mp3 players and the basis of this commentary. I am convinced that as you read and study with Scott, you will find Romans understandable and applicable. His frequent and appropriate use of cross-references to other texts helps clarify the truth Paul is teaching. You will come to understand the biblical doctrines so crucial to our Christian faith, not from a text on theology but from the only systematic presentation of theology in the Scripture, Paul's Epistle to the Romans, the "Constitution of Christianity."

As a fan and student of Romans for almost 40 years and a fan and student of Scott Gilchrist for 20 years, I highly recommend this readable commentary to all my friends and former students on both sides of the Atlantic and the Pacific! My hope is that just as Scott's teaching of Romans has been translated into several languages, this written commentary likewise will be translated. I know many pastors worldwide who would be thrilled and blessed as you will be as you read and study it.

Rev. Dr. Richard D. Calenberg, Th.D.
President, Evangelical Seminary of West Africa

PREFACE

It has been about a half-century (forty-nine years to be exact) since my life was greatly impacted by the book of Romans. I was a sophomore in college when I was challenged to give myself to the study of Romans. As I did so, I found myself understanding the gospel of Jesus Christ in a deeper way and desiring to proclaim that gospel with more boldness and clarity. I began to teach others the book of Romans and challenge them to give themselves to a firsthand study of this dynamic letter from the Apostle Paul to the believers at Rome.

Now all these years later, I still find myself encouraging others to saturate their minds and hearts in this amazing portion of God's inspired Word. Just this past week, a young pastor told me that as he is reading and rereading the book of Romans, he is grasping the great truths of the gospel in a fresh and new way.

Let me encourage you to read the entire book of Romans today. Read it in one sitting if you can. It only takes about 45 to 50 minutes. Then read it again. Repeated readings of this amazing epistle will pay great dividends in your walk with Christ and your grasp of just how magnificent the good news really is. Time after time, I have watched God get ahold of an individual's heart when he or she began to spend real, concentrated time in Romans.

I have had the privilege of teaching Romans in many different settings over the years, sometimes to large congregations and sometimes to a small number of interested Christians. About twenty years ago, I preached through Romans week by week in our morning worship service for over two years. God greatly used that in-depth study in the lives of many. Some understood the gospel of grace for the first time and put their trust in Christ Jesus as their Savior and Lord. Others found themselves deepening their understanding of their sinfulness and the corresponding wealth of the grace of God found in Christ. Many expressed a growing gratitude to our Lord for what He accomplished for us at the cross.

Some years later, I preached through Romans seeking to explain and teach it in fewer sessions. We experienced great blessing as a church just sweeping through Paul's logical argument in about twenty messages. In 2014 I was invited to teach a survey of Romans in this way to a large gathering of pastors and Christian leaders in Ethiopia. I taught the entire book of Romans in eighteen sessions over the course of five days. Those eighteen sessions have been translated into several African languages and have been widely distributed and listened to throughout many countries in Africa. God has seen fit to use that teaching in the lives of many to bring about the transformation that He speaks of when He says, "Be transformed by the renewing of your mind" (Romans 12:2).

This brief commentary is the product of those teaching sessions. I make no claim to eloquence or polish. They are edited transcripts of those sessions taught through an interpreter to the grateful gathering of Ethiopian pastors and leaders.

We continually hear from many that the Lord has used the verbal communication of this teaching, and to that end, we are now praying that He will bless the written communication of this teaching of Romans.

I pray that as you read the comments, you will be aided in your understanding of this wonderful portion of God's Word that we call "Romans." May you be encouraged, strengthened, and established in the amazing gospel, and may He embolden you to explain and proclaim this gospel to others.

Scott Gilchrist
Portland, Oregon

1

WHY ROMANS?

In Paul's day, all roads led to Rome. Although he longed to travel there, he had yet to do so. Unlike his other epistles, Paul does not have to deal with local issues in a church he has planted. Instead, he is able to systematically and clearly lay out the whole gospel in all its grandeur. Romans is perhaps the most formal of Paul's letters. I can imagine the great apostle carefully polishing his writing, thinking through what he had been preaching for a couple of decades by that point. It is like a lawyer building his case for Christianity. There is a grand sweep to it.

Romans has rightly been called "the Constitution of Christianity." It is foundational to the Christian faith, containing within this one epistle the doctrines of justification, sanctification, God's power for salvation, divine condemnation, divine election, and the revelation of God. You can see and hear the theme of the righteousness of God that the Gospel reveals and makes known throughout the whole letter. Martin Luther referred to Romans as "the purest Gospel." In the preface to his commentary on Romans, Luther wrote:

> "This epistle is really the chief part of the New Testament,
> and is truly the purest Gospel. It is worthy not only that

every Christian should know it word for word, by heart, but also that he should occupy himself with it every day, as the daily bread of the soul. We can never read it or ponder over it too much; for the more we deal with it, the more precious it becomes and the better it tastes."[1]

Romans Impact through history

God has greatly used Romans throughout history. St. Augustine was converted from a text in Romans. Martin Luther was transformed by it. "Romans left Luther undone by God's message of a totally free righteousness. It's the same message that lit a fire in Luther leading to the Reformation."[2] Through Luther's transformation, a whole continent was changed. Two hundred years later, John Wesley was listening to Luther's introduction to Romans, and his comments on Romans Chapter 1:17 and God struck his heart with the truth of the gospel. John Wesley and his brother Charles were greatly used both in Britain and in America to lead an awakening of the church, a great revival that swept through the English-speaking world. John had been previously ordained and had been a missionary, but he dated his conversion, his salvation, to hearing the gospel from Romans.

In my own life, I have been greatly influenced by John Mitchell, co-founder of Multnomah School of the Bible, now Multnomah University. As I got to know Mitchell, he told me of how the

---

1   Grunewald, R.J (2016). Reading Romans with Luther. Concordia Publishing House. St Louis, p. 9

2   *Id.*

book of Romans had impacted his life. Romans is about all he knew about the Bible when he initially went out to proclaim the gospel. He gave himself to Romans and found that as he went out and proclaimed the book of Romans, God changed lives. I can remember Mitchell stating, "You get well-established in Romans, and you're well established." I wanted to be well-established; I wanted to understand the gospel of grace, so I gave myself to Romans.

Being Established in Romans

Three things happen to anyone who gets established in the book of Romans:

1. There will be doctrinal stability. The church and Christians today are prone to be blown here and there. In the book of Ephesians, Paul writes *"we are no longer to be children, tossed here and there … and carried about by every wind of doctrine."*[3] There needs to be doctrinal stability in our lives. If you give yourself to Romans, you will understand the key truths of the Bible better and will not be just "weathervaning."

2. There will be a depth of conviction; not merely a creed you hold to or some doctrine that you hold to intellectually, but a depth of conviction where these truths become yours.

3. There will be real usefulness. God uses men and women who understand His grace and righteousness, where the gospel has truly gotten hold of them. Read Romans with the goal of asking God to deepen your convictions, and He will make you more and more fruitful for Him.

---

3   Ephesians 4:14

Study Questions

- Why do some consider Romans to be "the Constitution of Christianity"?

- What are the fruits of being well-grounded in the Book of Romans?

2

INTRODUCTION

Romans 1:1-17

Romans is perhaps the most polished of all the letters written by Paul. He does not go off on side issues; he stays focused on the gospel. In many of his letters, the introduction is only two or three verses. In Romans, the introduction is seventeen verses, the longest of all his letters. Paul's introductions are never just casual introductions because this is not Paul's word; this is God's Word. As previously stated, many people call the book of Romans the "Constitution of Christianity." Just as the Constitution has a preamble, we should look carefully at the introduction to Romans.

"The Gospel of God" — 1:1-7

1:1 *"Paul, a bond-servant of Christ Jesus, called as an apostle, set apart for the gospel of God,*

1:2 *which He promised beforehand through His prophets in the Holy Scriptures,*

1:3 *concerning His Son, who was born of the seed of David according to the flesh,*

> **1:4** *who was declared with power to be the Son of God by the resurrection from the dead, according to the Spirit of holiness, Jesus Christ our Lord,*
> **1:5** *through whom we have received grace and apostleship to bring about the obedience of faith among all the Gentiles for His name's sake,*
> **1:6** *among whom you also are the called of Jesus Christ;*
> **1:7** *to all who are beloved of God in Rome, called as saints: Grace to you and peace from God our Father and the Lord Jesus Christ."*

This is God's Word, but obviously it is written by Paul. Paul identifies himself right at the beginning as the human author. He does not call himself Paul the "Right Reverend" or the "Great Apostle." He begins, "Paul, a bond-servant, a slave of Christ Jesus."[4] We should all take our place as slaves of the Master. At the same time, he was "called as an apostle." Amazingly, God entrusts sinful men like you and me to places of leadership. Paul said I am the chief of sinners.[5] Yet he was called as an apostle, which means "sent one." I am not an apostle, but I am sent. We may not all be apostles, but we are all, every Christian, sent.

Paul took this seriously, and I believe we should too. When the word apostle is translated into Latin, we get the word "mission" and "missionary." Every one of us can take our place as a slave of Christ and a sent one. The verse continues, "set apart for the gospel." Our lives are to be devoted to the gospel. Paul

---

4   Romans 1:1
5   See I Timothy 1:15

saw himself as wholly set apart to the gospel. He tells us what he is going to write about in the first verse – "the gospel of God." This is the good news about God, the good news from God. Everything you learn about God is good news. Everything you know about God is gospel. It is good news; God is good. Every good thing comes from God. Paul grasps this in the very first line of Romans; I am "set apart for the gospel of God."[6]

This gospel was "promised beforehand" in the sacred writings, the Holy Scriptures, the Holy Bible.[7] The gospel is not something new. It is founded in the Old Testament. The Old and New Testaments fit together. God did not just come on the scene. He began to tell us about Himself from the very beginning when He created the heavens and the earth and created us male and female—the first page of the Bible. He promised through the centuries this gospel that Paul is going to explain, writing from a perspective of the 1st Century.

And, importantly, this gospel concerns "His Son."[8] The church should never forget that. You should never forget that. The gospel is not about good works. The gospel is not a bunch of data or information. The gospel is not even a philosophy. The gospel is about a person. It concerns Jesus Christ, His Son. We proclaim Christ because He is the gospel; what He did for us. Yes, explanation of the gospel includes a lot of important information. There are, after all, sixteen chapters in Romans. But the gospel's central concern is His Son, who was truly man,

---

6   Romans 1:1
7   Romans 1:2
8   Romans 1:3

"born of the seed of David,"[9] just like the Old Testament said. And, He is truly God, "Declared with power to be the Son of God by the resurrection from the dead, according to the Spirit of holiness."[10]

Paul's prayer to the Romans — 1:8-10

1:8 *"First, I thank my God through Jesus Christ for you all, because your faith is being proclaimed throughout the whole world.*

1:9 *For God, whom I serve in my spirit in the preaching of the gospel of His Son, is my witness as to how unceasingly I make mention of you,*

1:10 *always in my prayers making request, if perhaps now at last by the will of God I may succeed in coming to you."*

Verses 8 through 10 are part of Paul's prayer to the Romans, which can be a pattern for us. We can draw out seven characteristics from these few verses. First, Paul's prayer was marked by thanksgiving. "I thank my God,"[11] he writes when I hear what is happening in Rome. Paul's prayers were permeated with thanksgiving. When you pray for others—and Paul prayed for the Romans—thank God for them, first and foremost. Thank Him for what He is doing in their lives.

Second, Paul was conscious that his prayer came to God through Jesus Christ. "I thank my God through Jesus Christ."[12]

---

9   *Id.*
10   Romans 1:4
11   Romans 1:8
12   *Id.*

On the night our Savior took his disciples to Himself and prepared them for His leaving, He mentioned four times that they could pray in His name. "If you ask the Father for anything in My name, He will give it to you."[13] All real prayer is offered to God the Father through His Son. We have access to God in prayer because of Jesus Christ, and Paul mentions that here at the outset.

Third, he prayed without ceasing. "How unceasingly I make mention of you"[14] in my prayers. That is what Paul told us to do, "Pray without ceasing."[15] Using the same word, Paul later tells Timothy, "I constantly remember you in my prayers night and day."[16] Paul was not saying that every moment of every day he was praying. There are times when we devote ourselves to prayer, and there are times when we pray whenever we get the chance. The idea is that we should stay relentless in our prayers.

Fourth, he prayed personally. "I make mention of you."[17] Paul had never been to Rome, yet in Chapter 16, there are twenty-seven personal names of greeting. There is power in personal prayer, praying by name. Do not just pray for people in general; pray for individuals. Bring them before the Lord; bring them before the throne of grace by name.

---

13   John 16:23. See also, John 14:13-14; John 15:16.
14   Romans 1:9
15   1 Thessalonians 5:17
16   2 Timothy 1:3
17   Romans 1:9

Fifth, Paul prayed specifically. He wanted to get to Rome, and he prayed specifically, "making request" [18] that he could get there. The Bible says, "Be anxious for nothing, but in everything by prayer and supplication with thanksgiving let your requests be made known unto God."[19] God wants to be asked. "You do not have because you do not ask."[20] He says, "Ask, and it will be given to you."[21] Paul prayed specifically, and he prayed relentlessly.

Sixth, he prayed submissively. "Making request, if perhaps now at last by the will of God I may succeed in coming to you."[22] Even though we should go to the throne of grace repeatedly and specifically in prayer, we are talking to God Almighty. The supreme example of submissive prayer is our Lord Jesus Himself. He said, "Yet not My will, but Yours be done."[23]

And seventh, he prayed genuinely. You can fool me, and I can fool you; we can do quite a bit of bluffing in our prayer life. But you cannot fool the Lord. Paul said, "God is my witness as to how unceasingly I make mention of you." [24] He was genuine in his heart of prayer.

---

18   Romans 1:10
19   Philippians 4:6
20   James 4:2
21   Matthew 7:7; Luke 11:9
22   Romans 1:10
23   Luke 22:42
24   Romans 1:9

Paul's heart for the Romans — 1:11-13

> **1:11** *"For I long to see you in order that I may impart some spiritual gift to you, that you may be established;*
> **1:12** *that is, that I may be encouraged together with you while among you, each of us by the other's faith, both yours and mine.*
> **1:13** *I do not want you to be unaware, brethren, that often I have planned to come to you (and have been prevented thus far) in order that I may obtain some fruit among you also, even as among the rest of the Gentiles."*

You see Paul's shepherd's heart here. "I long to see you."[25] He wanted to get there. He had never been to Rome. He did not know these people personally, except those who had traveled to Rome that he had met in other parts of the empire. Yet, he had a longing for them. "I long ... to impart some spiritual gift to you, that you may be established."[26] Paul is not using the technical phrase that he could confer "spiritual gifts." We know that spiritual gifts come from the Holy Spirit. Paul is thinking of mutual benefit. He goes right on to explain, "that is, that I may be encouraged together with you ... each of us by the other's faith [the mutual faith], both yours and mine."[27] There was no "apostolic" lording it over them. You see Paul's humility that he might be encouraged by them, and they by him.

---

25 Romans 1:11
26 *Id.*
27 Romans 1:12

"I am not ashamed of the gospel" — 1:14-16

1:14 *"I am under obligation both to Greeks and to barbarians, both to the wise and to the foolish.*

1:15 *Thus, for my part, I am eager to preach the gospel to you also who are in Rome.*

1:16 *For I am not ashamed of the gospel, for it is the power of God for salvation to everyone who believes, to the Jew first and also to the Greek."*

Verses 14, 15, and 16 all start with the phrase, "I am." Paul says, "I am under obligation;" "I am eager;" "I am not ashamed (of the gospel)." Paul first states that he is "under obligation" to preach the gospel. He did not take this as an optional undertaking. We should not either. We are under obligation. Verse 14 goes on to make clear that the gospel is the great equalizer. Romans will teach that we are all in need of the gospel. Today more than ever, Africa, America, Europe, Asia all need the gospel. Everyone – male, female, rich, poor, wise, foolish, educated, uneducated, powerful, marginalized – all are lost without the gospel, and we can all be saved by the gospel. Paul says, to everyone who believes, Jews or Gentiles (the Greek), that covers all of us, we can all be saved by the gospel.

Paul continues, "I am eager to preach the gospel."[28] I ask the Lord to keep me "eager to teach the gospel," to proclaim the gospel and to use opportunities to tell people about the gospel. We may not all be called to "preach," but we are called to proclaim.

---

28   Romans 1:15

Paul next writes, "I am not ashamed of the gospel."[29] By saying that, I believe that Paul was tempted to be ashamed of the gospel, just like I am tempted, but he did not give in to that temptation. Why would we be ashamed of God's power? Because we are so sinful. Paul said, "I am not ashamed of the gospel." Why? – "for it is the power[30] of God for salvation."[31] There is a parallel verse where Paul again uses this term, "the power of God." When you find parallel passages in the Bible, it is good to study them; to learn all that we can. Paul writes in his letter to the Corinthians, "For the word of the cross is to those who are perishing foolishness, but to us who are being saved it is the power of God."[32] What is the power of God? The word of the cross. What is the power of God? The gospel. What is the gospel? The word of the cross. I proclaim "Jesus Christ, and Him crucified" [33] and risen from the dead.

We need to come back to the cross if we are to preach the gospel. The gospel is not just that Jesus was an example for us. Yes, He is the perfect example. He is what we should be as men and women. But if Jesus was only an example, if we are just to try to emulate Him, that is not good news because we all fall short. The good news is that Jesus Christ came "to give his life a ransom for many."[34] He said it over and over, it is necessary for the Son of Man to die.[35] He said he was born

29 Romans 1:16
30 *"Dunamis"* in New Testament Greek, which is where we get our words dynamic and dynamite.
31 Romans 1:16
32 1 Corinthians 1:18
33 *See* 1 Corinthians 2:2
34 Matthew 20:28; Mark 10:45
35 *See* Luke 9:22

to die; not for His sin, He had none, but for our sin. This is the word of the cross. "Unless a grain of wheat falls into the earth and dies, it remains by itself alone."[36] He said that in connection with saying He would be raised up on a stake and die for us. This is the gospel, the power of God, that Paul is not ashamed of, and we don't need to be either. The gospel is still saving men and women today.

"The righteousness of God" — 1:17

1:17 *"For in it the righteousness of God is revealed from faith to faith; as it is written, 'But the righteous man shall live by faith.'"*

"The righteousness of God" is the theme of Romans. Paul does not speak yet of the love of God. The great burden of Paul's gospel is "the righteousness of God." Sometimes people debate, is it God's attribute of righteousness, or is it His way of justifying sinners? Both. You cannot know one without the other. The righteousness of God speaks not only of His righteousness but that He declares righteous those who put their faith in Christ. In the gospel, the righteousness of God is declared to those who believe. Paul will explain the details of this righteousness of God in the rest of Romans.

This is what set Martin Luther free and millions of others since then. Since Paul began proclaiming this gospel, since Christ died and rose again, the righteousness of God is available to all who believe. When Martin Luther saw righteousness as just

36   John 12:24

the attribute of God, it depressed him. He knew that God was righteous and he knew that he was a sinner. He thought that the best way to overcome his sin was to become a monk. He tried to pay off his sin by fasting, praying, and being a good monk. Luther is reported to have said, "If ever a monk got to heaven by his monkery, it was I."[37] But he did not have freedom from his sin. Then in reading Romans, Luther saw that the righteousness of God is not only the attribute of God but that He declares righteous those who believe in his Son. Paul is going to say this again in Chapter 3 of Romans, that "for the demonstration … of His righteousness … that He might be just and the justifier of the one who has faith in Jesus."[38] Paul later states it this way: "He made Him who knew no sin, Jesus, to be sin on our behalf, that we might become the righteousness of God in Him."[39]

This is the gospel of Jesus Christ. This is the gospel that set Martin Luther free, set John Wesley free, set me free, set millions free. The righteous man lives by faith. When you come to believe in Jesus Christ, God charges the righteousness of Christ to your account. This is the gospel Paul is going to write about all through Romans. This is the gospel that Paul is not ashamed of and eager to proclaim. And this is how he introduced his letter to the Romans.

---

37 Bainton, R. (1950). *Here I Stand: A Life of Martin Luther*. New York, NY: Mentor, p. 34.
38 Romans 3:26
39 2 Corinthians 5:21

Study questions

- What is the gospel that Paul declares in this section?

- What lessons about prayer life can we learn from verses 1:8-10?

- Why was Paul "not ashamed of the gospel" (1:16)? How are you tempted to be ashamed of the gospel in your life?

- What is meant by "the righteousness of God?" in verse 1:17?

3
MAN'S UNRIGHTEOUSNESS
Romans 1:18-32

Paul ends his introduction to Romans with verse 17, the very theme of the gospel. "For in it the righteousness of God is revealed from faith to faith." How can a man, a sinner, be right with a righteous God? Through faith in the God who gave His Son on our behalf, in our place. That is the good news; that is the gospel. Paul is going to explain it in a number of chapters later in Romans. But Paul first begins his explanation of the good news with bad news – man's unrighteousness. We want to let it speak to our hearts because often people are not ready to hear the gospel because they have not heard the bad news. They have not understood the condition of their own heart.

The following verses begin the first major section of Romans – Paul's argument. This is where it starts. In an outline, this would be Romans numeral one: verses 1:18 through 3:20 – Man's Unrighteousness.

1:18 *"For the wrath of God is revealed from heaven against all ungodliness and unrighteousness of men who suppress the truth in unrighteousness,*
1:19 *because that which is known about God is evident within them; for God made it evident to them.*
1:20 *For since the creation of the world His invisible attributes, His eternal power and divine nature, have been clearly seen, being understood through what has been made, so that they are without excuse.*
1:21 *For even though they knew God, they did not honor Him as God or give thanks; but they became futile in their speculations, and their foolish heart was darkened.*
1:22 *Professing to be wise, they became fools,*
1:23 *and exchanged the glory of the incorruptible God for an image in the form of corruptible man and of birds and four-footed animals and crawling creatures."*

Looking at the news both locally and internationally, a thoughtful person has to ask the question, is this the way it was meant to be? When you look at the personal lives of the people you live and work with, at your own life, you see the pointlessness, the emptiness, the brokenness of the closest relationships, and the resulting heartache and bitterness. When you read the news, hear it on television, you hear of rape, murder, deceit, abuse, divorce, and addictions. Is this the way it should be? What went wrong?

Paul begins the good news by explaining the condition of man. Before looking at this section verse by verse, a quick synopsis would be — man's great problem is wrong thinking about God.

And wrong thinking about God leads to wrong thinking about man. This wrong thinking is not arrived at innocently; we are without excuse. God will hold us accountable for our sins.

Paul begins this section on man's unrighteousness as a lawyer would. Paul had been preaching the gospel for many years. This is his logical argument for the gospel. It is like a lawyer's legal brief if you will. In that way, Paul is a lot like the Old Testament prophets Isaiah, Jeremiah, and Hosea. They were often called upon to be a prosecuting attorney. They had God's holy law, and they convicted Israel of breaking that law. Paul begins with what you can think of as an indictment, which he starts in verse 18 and goes all the way to Chapter 3:20.

To change the analogy, if we are erecting a building, these verses are the foundation. Before you can build the super-structure of the gospel, there must be a foundation. But this is not even the foundation. Before you can lay a foundation, you must first excavate — do the "dirt work." You do not pour a foundation on top of muck, roots, and the debris that is there. You have to remove all that and get down to a base. Before Paul gives us the foundation of Jesus Christ, "for no man can lay a foundation other than that which is laid, which is Jesus Christ,"[40] he does this excavation, this dirt work. Paul wants us to abandon trust in our own righteousness. We are not ready for the foundation until we get over ourselves.

We do not like doing "dirt work." It is messy and unpleasant. For this reason, many people do not even like to read

---

40   1 Corinthians 3:11

Chapters 1 and 2 and the first part of Chapter 3 of Romans. I was leading a bible study with a prominent athletic coach, and he said he wanted me to take him through Romans. As we were in this section, he said, "I don't like it." I said, "You're not supposed to like it; you're supposed to listen to it." The first step in understanding the good news is to get the excavation done, to abandon hope in man. By nature, we are proud and trust in ourselves. The gospel takes away that trust and that self-reliance. If you get Romans Chapters 1, 2, and 3 right, so much else falls into place. If you get the excavation done, the foundation can be laid firm and steady.

Let me change the analogy, yet again, from a legal brief to construction of a building, to seeing a doctor. We generally do not go to the doctor until we are sick. You go to a doctor, and he gives a diagnosis of the problem. Jesus Christ is the great Physician. Before we are ready to take the medicine and have treatment, we need our problem diagnosed.

"The wrath of God" – 1:18

This section begins with verse 18, "For the wrath of God is revealed from heaven against all ungodliness and unrighteousness of men, who suppress the truth in unrighteousness." "Wrath" is the first word of Paul's argument. Paul is not ashamed of wrath; he uses the term twelve times in Romans. Worse yet, this is the wrath of God. Paul is not embarrassed to proclaim a God of wrath. The God of the Bible is a righteous God. He has deep, personal abhorrence of evil.

God's wrath "is revealed."[41] This is in the present tense. The wrath of God is revealed now – in the present. That does not preclude a future wrath of God. But Paul begins by saying the wrath of God is currently, presently revealed against sin. God's wrath is presently being revealed in at least three ways: First, this world is wrong, it is not right. There is suffering, heartache, and betrayal. Secondly, God's wrath has fallen at various times throughout biblical history. For example, He brought about the flood of Noah's day. Sodom and Gomorrah became so wicked that they were judged by God. And He brought punishment when Korah rebelled against God and His leadership. Thirdly, wrath is presently revealed ultimately through what happened at the cross. When man's sin was placed on his beloved Son, judgment fell. "My God, My God, why have You forsaken Me?"[42] "He made Him who knew no sin to be sin on our behalf."[43] He became an accursed thing on the cross.[44] God has not changed; He still hates sin.

The God of the Bible is presently revealing His wrath against sin. This wrath of God is personal, and it is deserved. Paul is laboring to prove that in the first two and a half chapters. In verse 18, Paul describes the whole human race as ungodly with no desire or reverence towards God. A godlessness if you will. This leads to active unrighteousness. Paul does not call us truth-seekers in this paragraph but rather truth suppressors.

---

41   Romans 1:18
42   Matthew 27:46
43   2 Corinthians 5:21
44   Galatians 3.13

Knowledge of God — 1:19-21

In these following verses, Paul echoes Genesis. History began with knowledge of God. Adam and Eve knew God, but they sinned. What was their sin? Basically, they went it alone. They said they could be wise in their own eyes. They could choose their own path. They went their own way and doing so resulted in death. Wisdom says: "Trust in the Lord with all your heart, and do not lean on your own understanding."[45] "Do not be wise in your own eyes; Fear the Lord and turn away from evil."[46]

Our problem is not that we did not know God. It is that we did not want to know God. Man's problem is that he doesn't want to honor God as God. Man's problem is a heart problem. God is God. Man doesn't want to give thanks to God or give Him worship and praise. Turn that around; our main responsibility in life is to worship God and give Him thanks and praise. The earmark of a Christian is gratitude.

Man's futile speculations – 1:21-23

Romans 1:21 ends by noting that man (the whole human race) willfully turns away from God's revelation. He begins to speculate about God. Man makes up his own ideas about God, and he is proud of it. In verse 22, man is "professing to be wise"; God's appraisal of this in the second half of the verse is that they are fools! Verse 23 goes on to state, they "exchanged the glory of the incorruptible God for an image in the form of corruptible man and of birds and four-footed animals and

---

45   Proverbs 3:5
46   Proverbs 3:7

crawling creatures." Notice how foolish the exchange is. Paul uses the term "exchange" twice. Verse 25 says man exchanged the truth of God for a lie. What is the lie? Worshipping and serving anything or anyone other than the one and only true God.

There are many examples. Ancient tribalism and paganism worship animals, rocks, mountains, trees, and rivers. Or look at the so-called great religions of the world. Hinduism, for instance, has over 300 million gods. And there is "Modern Thought." In the West, we have "evolutionary scientism" (I call it not science but "scientism"). Those who espouse this view ultimately bow down and worship just matter and time, some mindless process that just keeps going. They will not even entertain the idea of design behind it, even though everywhere you look you, see design. They say, "no, it's all random." All these are sad examples of turning away from God and his revelation to our own speculations. God hates it. He is a jealous God. He wants to be worshipped as the one and only true God.

In Isaiah Chapter 44, we see the cutting comments God makes to His prophets regarding the folly, the foolishness, of making up your own god. The people would take a piece of wood and cut it in half. They would carve one half into an object of worship and hire the best goldsmith and craftsman to make it beautiful, being careful that it would not totter. They would then fall down and worship it. Meanwhile, they would warm their hands and cook their food over a fire with the other half of the log.[47] You fools, He said. It is sad and tragic. Whatever

---

47   *See* Isaiah 44: 9-20; Isaiah 40:19-20

brand of rebellion you pick, whether one of the great religions or man's evolutionary pomp, it is very tragic and sad.

"God gave them over" — 1:24-28

In verses 24 through 28, Paul says, "God gave them over" ("God lets them"). Three times he said it, verses 24, 26, and 28. Man turns away from God and God lets him.

> **1:24** *"Therefore God gave them over in the lusts of their hearts to impurity, that their bodies might be dishonored among them.*
>
> **1:25** *For they exchanged the truth of God for a lie, and worshiped and served the creature rather than the Creator, who is blessed forever. Amen.*
>
> **1:26** *For this reason God gave them over to degrading passions; for their women exchanged the natural function for that which is unnatural,*
>
> **1:27** *and in the same way also the men abandoned the natural function of the woman and burned in their desire toward one another, men with men committing indecent acts and receiving in their own persons the due penalty of their error.*
>
> **1:28** *And just as they did not see fit to acknowledge God any longer, God gave them over to a depraved mind, to do those things which are not proper."*

God gave them over to impurity, to degrading passions, and to a depraved mind. It is not easy to read. It is sad, but it is real. The condition of the human race is a direct result of turning away from God. We must specifically address verses 26 and 27 because there is a great need to hear what God says about the dishonoring of our bodies and the sad tragedy of homosexual and lesbian behavior. Paul addresses it here at the beginning of the gospel. We can say several things from these two verses. First, this behavior is sinful. There are those who will say, "Yes, but they were born this way. These are just their natural desires." I will not argue against that; I will just say, "Yes, ever since Adam and Eve sinned, we are born with evil tendencies." The thief has a natural inclination to steal. The liar has a natural inclination to deceive. There is selfishness and hate in us that lead to murder. The heterosexual adulterer says, "I just desire that." The Bible does not argue the case; it just says that is wrong. Even in human courts, you will not get off by saying, "I was just born that way, to steal things."

Others claim this behavior is a result of their environment, something that happened in their life. Again, the biblical answer is, "yes, it is environmental." As we have turned further from God and indulged the lusts of the flesh, we become more and more depraved – this is our environment. Ever since Adam sinned, we do not think right; we do not think clearly. God gave the whole race over to a depraved mind.

At the same time, we need to remember, as Christians, and I want to underline this, when we talk of sin, specific sin, like Paul does, always we proclaim the gospel for sinners. Christ Jesus came into the world to save sinners. No matter what the sin. "Christ Jesus came into the world to save sinners, among whom I am foremost of all."[48]

"Filled with all unrighteousness" — *1:29-32*
Paul then fills in the details in verses 29 and following:

> **1:29** *"Being filled with all unrighteousness, wickedness, greed, evil; full of envy, murder, strife, deceit, malice; they are gossips,*
> **1:30** *slanderers, haters of God, insolent, arrogant, boastful, inventors of evil, disobedient to parents,*
> **1:31** *without understanding, untrustworthy, unloving, unmerciful;*
> **1:32** *and although they know the ordinance of God, that those who practice such things are worthy of death, they not only do the same, but also give hearty approval to those who practice them."*

This is what we are full of, all unrighteousness, all the sins, set forth in verses 29 and 30. In every culture in the world, wherever you go, you will find the race permeated with these kinds of things. Paul shifts gear a bit and in verse 31, he says we lack understanding, we are untrustworthy, unloving, and unmerciful. This is an accurate diagnosis of the human race. And right in the center of it, verse 30, we are "haters of God."

I say again, the thoughtful person looks at the condition of the human race and asks, "Is this the way that it should be?" The

48 1 Timothy 1:15

Bible does not say, "Yes, it's pretty good; we just need a little help." The Bible answers, "No, this is not the way it should be." All these problems arise from wrong thinking about the God of Revelation. Those wrong ideas about God lead to wrong ideas about man and what life is all about. And those wrong ideas are not innocent, "we are without excuse."[49] Man turns away from God and God lets him. We know in our hearts that we are worthy of death, and we should not do these things, but we do them anyway.

In the midst of this, it is hard not to look ahead. Romans goes on to explain that "all have sinned and fall short of the glory of God."[50] This is us. "For the wages of sin is death,"[51] but that is not the whole message. The sentence goes on, "but the free gift of God is eternal life in Christ Jesus our Lord."[52] We should never be ashamed of the good news. In the flow of Romans, however, Paul is not there yet. He is still arguing the case of our need for the gospel.

---

49   Romans 1:20
50   Romans 3:23
51   Roman 6:23
52   *Id.*

Study questions

- Why does Paul begin this section mentioning "The wrath of God?" How is God's wrath being presently revealed?

- How does God's creation give all humanity knowledge of Him?

- How has humanity turned away from their knowledge of God? Think of examples today of how people professing to be wise have become fools (2:22)?

- Give examples of man's unrighteousness described by Paul in verses 1:29-32.

4

GOD'S RIGHTEOUS JUDGMENT

Romans 2:1-16

Sometimes people argue against the gospel because of all the evil in the world. That does not argue against the gospel; it argues *for* the gospel. This world is evil. It is full of problems, given over to impurity and depravity of mind. This is not the way it should be. This is the present revelation of God's wrath against man's sin. By beginning his epistle there, referring to the present tense judgment of God against sin, Paul is in no way arguing against the future judgment of God against sin.

In the first 16 verses of Romans chapter two, Paul is indicting the self-righteous "good person." We will see seven principles of God's righteous judgment that are particularly devastating to self-righteousness. Self-righteousness so quickly rears its ugly head. It is our tendency to self-justify and to consider ourselves righteous. Perhaps our most prevalent sin is self-righteousness – self-justification. Chapter 2 starts: "Therefore, you are without excuse, every one of you who passes judgment, for in that which you judge another, you condemn yourself;

for you who judge practice the same things."[53] You and I have a natural tendency to self-justify and point a finger at others. As Paul gave that awful list of sin at the end of Chapter 1, we might think, "I've never done some of those things." You can always find somebody who, you believe, is worse than yourself, and so at the end of Romans Chapter 1, it is easy for the religious person or the moral person to say, "Oh yes, that is awful." But Paul is like a prosecuting attorney; he says, "No, therefore, you are without excuse.'"

You can see the tightness of his logic here. In Romans Chapter 1, Paul was speaking of the whole human race; "they" knew God. "They" refused him. Twenty-three times "they" is used in Chapter 1. In Chapter 2, however, Paul says "you"! In the first five verses of Chapter 2, he uses the "you" or "your" pronoun fifteen times. In the whole chapter, he uses "you" thirty-one times. If you have escaped the gross sin of Chapter 1, do not start to congratulate yourself.

In the first part of Chapter 2, Paul explains seven principles of God's righteous judgment on all of us. This could probably be narrowed down to simply saying that God's judgment is righteous and impartial. But Paul delineates it so that it helps convict us of our sin.

---

53   Romans 2:1

First Principle: God's Judgment is according to truth

2:1 *"Therefore, you are without excuse, every one of you who passes judgment, for in that which you judge another, you condemn yourself; for you who judge practice the same things.*

2:2 *And we know that the judgment of God rightly falls upon those who practice such things."*

Ours is a day of deceit. We deceive others. We end up deceiving ourselves. Sometimes we refer to this as "spin." But God is not fooled. God is the God of truth, and His judgment is according to the truth. God desires "truth in the innermost being."[54] Jesus prayed, "Sanctify them in the truth; Your word is truth."[55] There will be no inaccuracies. Everything God says, every judgment He makes, will be true.

Second Principle: God's judgment is Righteous

2:3 *"And do you suppose this, O man, when you pass judgment on those who practice such things and do the same yourself, that you will escape the judgment of God?*

2:4 *Or do you think lightly of the riches of His kindness and forbearance and patience, not knowing that the kindness of God leads you to repentance?*

---

54   Psalms 51:6
55   John 17:17. *See also* John 14:6

2:5 *But because of your stubbornness and your unrepentant heart you are storing up wrath for yourself in the day of wrath and revelation of the righteous judgment of God,"*

In the last phrase of verse 5, Paul refers to "the righteous judgment" of God. Jesus is righteous. He never makes mistakes. The Psalmist says, His judgments are "righteous altogether."[56] He is the Supreme Court. There will be no Court of Appeals. This brings confidence and joy to believers and terror to unbelievers. For believers, the Bible says, "as He is, so also are we in this world."[57] This gives us great confidence because we have found righteousness in Christ.

Third Principle: God's Judgment is inevitable

God's judgment is absolutely inevitable. Do not think, he says, that you will somehow escape it. "Do you suppose this, O man," verse 3 says, "when you pass judgment [upon others] ..., that you will escape the Judgment of God?" Or verse 4, "do you think lightly of the riches of His kindness and forbearance and patience?" Do not mistake His kindness for weakness. Do not assume that because His judgment has not yet fallen, that it will not. Do not mistake His patience for unwillingness to judge. The end of verse 4 says, His patience is designed to lead us to repentance. Do not think lightly of His kindness, His patience is waiting, "not wishing for any to perish but for all to come to repentance."[58]

---

56   Psalms 19:9.
57   1 John 4:17
58   2 Peter 3:9

It is very common to think wrongly about these things. In verse 3, Paul says, "do you suppose," and the word he uses here is, do you "think," do you "reckon," that God will not judge? We think wrong. Recall how in Chapter 1, Paul says He "gave us over" to a wrong mind; we think wrong. To think lightly of these riches, verse 4, is to miscalculate. In lesser matters of life, we often miscalculate. Paul says, do not think that you will ever escape the Judgment of God – you are miscalculating. Verse 5 says that by so doing, you are storing up wrath in the Day of Judgment. God's patience is like a great dam that holds back his wrath. But in the sweep of the Biblical revelation, always that inevitable, inescapable judgment awaits.

Fourth principle: God's Judgment is according to reality

God's judgment will be according to deeds, not mere profession or appearance. In other words, God's judgment will not be for what we *said,* but for what we *did,* who we are.

> **2:6** *"[God] who will render to every man according to his deeds:*
> **2:7** *to those who by perseverance in doing good seek for glory and honor and immortality, eternal life;*
> **2:8** *but to those who are selfishly ambitious and do not obey the truth, but obey unrighteousness, wrath and indignation.*
> **2:9** *There will be tribulation and distress for every soul of man who does evil, of the Jew first and also of the Greek,*

> **2:10** *but glory and honor and peace for everyone who does good, to the Jew first and also to the Greek.*
> **2:11** *For there is no partiality with God."*

Verse 6 states, "God will render to every man according to his deeds." Verses 7 through 11 expand on this. We are often mistaken on this issue. The church often misrepresents it. As Christians, we have found grace, unmerited favor. We sometimes forget that God's judgment, on the other hand, is merited. In the Bible, salvation is always according to Grace. Judgment is always according to merit. Many people tell me, "I believe God will judge me according to how I have lived (my deeds)." I tell them, "He will. And if He judges according to deeds, and He does, you're in trouble."

Note, however, Paul is *not* talking about salvation in these verses. He is talking about the judgment of God rightly falling on unrighteous people. Verses 7 through 11 speak about life choices. Paul is not yet talking about how to be justified. He is not yet talking about attaining eternal life. That will come later in Chapter 3 and the following. Rather, here Paul is describing those who do evil and those who show the reality of their faith in Jesus by doing good. In solemn truth, the unsaved will be judged by their deeds – Jews and Gentiles.[59] "For there is no partiality with God."[60]

---

59   Romans 2:9
60   Romans 2:11

Fifth principle: Judgment will be according to the light a man has; Not according to what he doesn't have.

2:12 *"For all who have sinned without the Law will also perish without the Law, and all who have sinned under the Law will be judged by the Law;*

2:13 *for it is not the hearers of the Law who are just before God, but the doers of the Law will be justified.*

2:14 *For when Gentiles, who do not have the Law do instinctively the things of the Law, these, not having the Law, are a law for themselves,*

2:15 *in that they show that the work of the Law written in their hearts, their conscience bearing witness, and their thoughts alternately accusing or else defending them,"*

Those who have been given more light, more responsibility, will be held to a stricter accountability. No one will be held to a higher standard than he should be. You can read "Bible" for "Law" in this section to better understand what is being said. In Paul's day, he would have said that an Israelite with all the scripture was more guilty than a Gentile who had never been given the Word of God. But none will escape judgment. Paul is saying that all who have sinned without the Law will perish without the Law. All who have sinned under the Law will be judged under the Law.

Paul is not talking about merely hearing God's law but acting on it. "For it is not the hearers of the Law who are just before God, but the doers of the Law will be justified."[61] The whole

---

61   Romans 2:13

gospel is to point us to the obedience of faith. Romans begins and ends with that phrase. Paul begins in Chapter 1 declaring that the gospel is "to bring about the obedience of faith among all the Gentiles [to all the nations]."[62] He will close with the same truth; the gospel "has been made known to all the nations, leading to obedience of faith."[63]

We are responsible to God. He has given us the external witness of His creation and the internal witness of our ability to grasp the external — our conscience. It is God given. But our conscience is not a sure guide. It is not totally accurate. The Bible says it can be "seared." Paul writes Timothy about men whose consciences are seared as with a branding iron.[64] We can cause our conscience to be dulled or calloused. We all fail to live up to our conscience. With or without a Bible, no one gets through life without failing to follow their conscience. Paul says in verse 15, "their conscience bearing witness, and their thoughts alternately accusing or else defending."

Sixth principle: God's judgment will be absolutely thorough

> **2:16** *"on the day when, according to my gospel, God will judge the secrets of men through Christ Jesus."*

This is a chilling thought – "the secrets of men." I can hide my sin from you. You can hide your sin from me. God's judgment,

---

62   Romans 1:5
63   Romans 16:26
64   1 Timothy 4:2

however, will judge everything; every thought, word, deed. I often ask men, what if I had a recording of everything you thought about for just the last 24 hours and I were to show it on a large screen. Their response — "Oh, please don't!"

The last statement in the book of Ecclesiastes states, "God will bring every act to judgment, everything which is hidden, whether it's good or evil."[65] And Jesus said,

> *"But there is nothing covered up that will not be revealed, and hidden that will not be known. Accordingly, whatsoever you have said in the dark will be heard in the light, and what you have whispered in the inner rooms will be proclaimed upon the housetops."*[66]

Seventh principle: His judgment will be through Jesus Christ

"On the day when, according to my gospel, God will judge the secrets of men through Christ Jesus."[67] Properly understood this should make us shudder more than any other principle. If you believe that Jesus is just a meek lamb who will never judge anyone, you have not seen the Jesus Christ of the Bible. Those who spurn Jesus Christ as Savior will face Him as Judge. "[God] has fixed a day in which He will judge the world in righteousness through a Man whom He has appointed, having furnished proof to all men by raising Him from the dead."[68] As

65   Ecclesiastes 12:14
66   Luke 12:2-3
67   Romans 2.16
68   Acts 17:31

Jesus Himself said, "For not even the Father judges anyone, but He has given all judgment to the Son, in order that all may honor the Son even as they honor the Father."[69]

In the book of Revelation, His eyes penetrate "like a flame of fire."[70] And yes, praise God, He is the Lamb. In fact, He is called the Lamb over thirty times in Revelation. But later in Revelation, we see a sobering description of all the presidents, and all the kings and all the dictators, and all the rich men, and every slave and every free man, every high person, every low person, fearing "the wrath of the Lamb":

> "Then the kings of the earth and the great men and the commanders and the rich and the strong and every slave and free man hid themselves in the caves and among the rocks of the mountains; and they said to the mountains and to the rocks, 'Fall on us and hide us from the presence of Him who sits on the throne, and from the wrath of the Lamb; for the great day of their wrath has come and who is able to stand?'"[71]

This describes a prayer meeting. They are calling out, but not to God. They are calling out to the mountains and the earth to hide them from the wrath of the Lamb. Every person will either know Jesus Christ as savior or face Him as Judge. "Therefore, also God highly exalted Him, and bestowed on Him the name which is above every name, that at the name of Jesus every

---

69   John 5:22-23
70   Revelation 1:14
71   Revelation 6:15-17

knee will bow, of those who are in heaven and on earth and under the earth."[72]

There is no question who Jesus Christ is in heaven. There is no question who Jesus is in hell. The whole creation knows and groans awaiting Jesus Christ.[73] The only place where there is any question of who He is, is in the sinful hearts of men. That is why I say, properly understood, this final principle of God's judgment is the most sobering. When I walk down the streets of where I live, if I am going to the office, or I overhear talk in "the locker rooms," I hear the name of Jesus Christ more often in blasphemy than in reverent worship.

We have not yet come to the good news. Under the inspiration of the Holy Spirit, Paul is writing out the gospel, the good news. But first, he is spending time on the bad news to help us see our great need of a Savior. I conclude the chapter with this thought, praise God for the gospel. It is the "power of God for salvation to everyone who believes, to the Jew first and also to the Greek." For in it the righteousness of God is revealed from faith to faith; as it is written, 'but the righteous man will live by faith.'"[74]

---

72 Philippians 2:9-10
73 *See* Romans 8:22
74 Romans 1:16-17

Study questions

- What is Paul's indictment against the self-righteous man who passes judgment on others?

- What principles are revealed in these verses about God's righteous judgment?

- Why should the non-believer fear that judgment will be "through Jesus Christ" (2:16)?

5

THE VERDICT IS GIVEN

Romans 2:17-29; 3:1-20

Paul has made clear that *all* men – the whole race – are without excuse. This is true not only of the openly unrighteous that Paul described in Chapter 1, but also the self-righteous in Chapter 2 — those of us who might think of ourselves a little less defiled, the moralist, or the so-called "good person."

In the rest of Chapter 2, verses 17 to the end, Paul addresses the self-righteous Jew or religionist. This can be further divided into two sections: the Jew or the religionist who trusts in the Law and self-righteousness in keeping the Law, verses 17-23, and the Jewish person or religionist who trusts in rituals or rites, verses 24-27. In other words, Paul takes on the two great pillars of the typical religious person's trust. Jews tended to trust in the Law and circumcision. Paul is laboring in his indictment to expose that as a false trust. It is a hypocritical trust. The Jews boasted in the Law, but they did not keep it. They boasted and trusted in circumcision, but circumcision was a sign of the righteousness that Abraham received by faith. Although Paul is speaking to the Jews with their laws and their circumcision, the principle applies to all who trust in their religion, rather than God Himself, including those who call themselves Christians.

False trust in the Law – 2:17-23

2:17 *"But if you bear the name 'Jew,' and rely upon the Law, and boast in God,*

2:18 *and know His will, and approve the things that are essential, being instructed out of the Law,*

2:19 *and are confident that you yourself are a guide to the blind, a light to those who are in darkness,*

2:20 *a corrector of the foolish, a teacher of the immature, having in the Law the embodiment of knowledge and of the truth,*

2:21 *you, therefore, who teach another, do you not teach yourself? You who preach that one should not steal, do you steal?*

2:22 *You who say that one should not commit adultery, do you commit adultery? You who abhor idols, do you rob temples?*

2:23 *You who boast in the Law, through your breaking the Law, do you dishonor God?*

The Hypocrisy of the Jews' (or the religionists') trust in the Law leaves them without excuse. There are many who go under the name of Christian who trust in keeping the Ten Commandments. This is a measure of the depravity of man's mind; how we treat God's Law. God gave the Law to drive us to Himself, to see our need for Christ. Paul says in Galatians, "the Law has become our tutor to lead us to Christ."[75] The Law is designed to destroy self-confidence. I cannot keep the first commandment, to love God with everything I have.[76] By the way, I can't keep the 10th commandment either, "you shall not covet."[77] Paul uses this later as an illustration in Chapter 7. Which one among us could say, "I have never coveted?"

The Law was given to destroy self-confidence. And yet the religionist uses the Law to prop up self-confidence. "I am doing my best to keep the laws." He is proud of his law-keeping. It is one of those great illustrations of the twistedness of man's thinking. Just like Paul wrote in Chapter 1 when we turned away from God, God gave us over to a depraved mind. We do not think clearly. God's sword of the Spirit helps us to see.[78]

False trust in rituals or circumcision – 2:24-27

2:24 *"For 'The name of God is blasphemed among the Gentiles because of you,' just as it is written.*
2:25 *For indeed circumcision is of value if you practice the Law; but if you are a transgressor of the Law, your circumcision has become uncircumcision.*
2:26 *If therefore the uncircumcised man keeps the requirements of the Law, will not his uncircumcision be regarded as circumcision?*

---

75   Galatians 3:24
76   *See* Deuteronomy 6:5; Matthew 22:37
77   Exodus 20:17
78   *See* Ephesians 6:17

> **2:27** *And he who is physically uncircumcised, if he keeps the Law, will he not judge you who though having the letter of the Law and circumcision are a transgressor of the Law?*

Paul says that all who trust in their religion are vulnerable to three sins: <u>pride</u>, "confident that you yourself are a guide to the blind and a light to those who are in darkness,"[79]; <u>greed</u>, "You who preach that one should not steal, do you steal?";[80] and <u>immorality</u>, "You who say that one should not commit adultery, do you commit adultery?"[81] Religion has no real power to deliver from the sin that so entangles us. The very things that God told the kings of Israel to avoid: pride, greed, immorality — multiplying horses, multiplying wives, multiplying gold and silver.[82] How many pastors have destroyed their testimony through one of these three areas? Ritualist religion will never deliver from the power of sin.

"That which is in the heart" – 2:28-29

The reality is what God is looking for is a heart issue:

> **2:28** *"For he is not a Jew who is one outwardly, neither is circumcision that which is outward in the flesh.*
> **2:29** *But he is a Jew who is one inwardly; and circumcision is that which is of the heart, by the Spirit, not by the letter; and his praise is not from men, but from God."*

---

79   Romans 2:19
80   Romans *2:21*
81   Romans 2:22.
82   *See* Deuteronomy 17:16-17

The Jews gloried in the outward ritual of circumcision. Millions of Christians glory in outward rituals of baptism, catechism, confirmation, or some other religious attainment. But God was never after just the outward ritual, even with circumcision. Paul says circumcision is of the heart. This is not an invention by Paul. The Old Testament often calls for circumcision of the heart. Deuteronomy states this in the negative, "circumcise your heart, and stiffen your neck no more."[83] To be circumcised of the heart is the opposite of being stiff-necked, stubborn, arrogant, or self-confident. Deuteronomy later states this positively, "Moreover the Lord your God will circumcise your heart and the heart of your descendants, to Love the Lord your God with all your heart and with all your soul, in order that you may live."[84] Circumcision of the heart is to love the Lord your God with all you have. "Watch over your heart with all diligence, for from it flow the springs of life."[85]

The prophet Jeremiah writes, "Circumcise yourselves to the Lord and remove the foreskins of your heart."[86] Jeremiah later writes what we should really boast in, not our riches or fame, but in knowing the Lord. It is a matter of the circumcision of the heart.

> *"Thus says the Lord, 'Let not a wise man boast of his wisdom, and let not the mighty man boast of his might, let not a rich man boast of his riches; but let him who boasts boast of this, that he understands and knows*

---

83 Deuteronomy 10:16
84 Deuteronomy 30:6
85 Proverbs 4:23
86 Jeremiah 4:4

Me, that I am the Lord who exercises lovingkindness, justice and righteousness on earth; for I delight in these things,' declares the Lord. 'Behold the days are coming,' declares the Lord, 'that I will punish all who are circumcised and yet uncircumcised – Egypt and Judah, and Edom and the sons of Ammon, and Moab ... for all the nations are uncircumcised, and all the house of Israel are uncircumcised of heart."[87]

Jeremiah parallels this section of Romans where Paul wants to get at the heart issue and cut away our self-reliance, whether it is based on morality or religiousness.

What is the advantage of being a Jew? – 3:1-2

3:1 *"Then what advantage has the Jew? Or what is the benefit of circumcision?*

3:2 *Great in every respect. First of all, that they were entrusted with the oracles of God."*

Paul has cut out from under the Jews their two pillars of self-righteousness: The Law and circumcision. He then raises the question, "Well then, what is the advantage of the Jew?"[88] Anyone who reads the Bible will wrestle with that issue. God gave us the Scripture through the Jews, and God gave many promises to the Jews through the Scripture. He is the God of Abraham, Isaac, and Jacob, and He is not done with Israel. Paul does not answer the question here in detail, but he will

---

87   Jeremiah 9:23-26
88   *See* Romans 3:1

expand on the blessings to Israel later in Romans Chapters 9, 10, and 11.

Paul then goes on to ask three more questions that continue to be asked today. This was Paul's teaching method. He knew the questions and the answers because he had been preaching and talking with people throughout the Roman empire. He dialogues with the questioner, if you will. It is part of the logic of Romans. The following questions and responses can also be seen as Paul the apostle arguing with Paul the Pharisee (or we should say, Saul the Pharisee). We should not forget that before coming to Christ, Paul was deep in religion and unbelief. He hated Christ. He had paperwork to drag Christians out of their homes and kill them. And in amazing grace, he met the risen Christ.

First question, will unbelief nullify or cancel God's faithfulness? – 3:3-4

> **3:3** *"What then? If some did not believe, their unbelief will not nullify the faithfulness of God, will it?*
> **3:4** *May it never be! Rather, let God be found true, though every man be found a liar, as it is written, 'That you may be justified in your words, and may prevail when you are judged.'"*

Paul is asking if a lot of people do not believe, will that nullify or cancel what God has said? Paul answers in verse 4, *Me genoito!* May it never be! Absolutely not! The majority of people in the United States and throughout the world do not believe in the God of the Bible. Will man's unbelief somehow change reality? Does that mean that God will not be faithful to His Word? *Me genoito!* God will accomplish His Word whether man believes it or not.

There are currently over seven billion people in the world. Even if everybody voted seven billion to one, "We don't believe in God," God still wins. He is God. God is true, and His Word is true. In economics, politics, social matters, in just about every area of life, majority thinking is often wrong. This is particularly true in eternal matters, spiritual matters, in our relationship with God. Jesus said, "Heaven and earth will pass away, but My words will not pass away."[89] "Enter through the narrow gate; for the gate is wide and the way is broad that leads to destruction."[90] It is like a freeway with many people on it. But "the gate is small and the way is narrow that leads to life, and few are those who find it."[91] We should not take votes on eternal matters.

Second question, is it wrong of God to demonstrate His righteousness through our unrighteousness? – 3:5-6

> **3:5** *"But if our unrighteousness demonstrates the righteousness of God, what shall we say? The God who inflicts wrath is not unrighteous, is He? (I am speaking in human terms.)*

---

89   Matthew 24:35
90   Mathew 7:13
91   Matthew 7:14

3:6 *May it never be! For otherwise, how will God judge the world?"*

I am sure Paul heard this question repeatedly as he proclaimed the gospel. This question comes in different forms. How can God be righteous with all the unrighteousness in the world? If God is God, why does He not just eradicate evil? Is it not wrong of God to show his righteousness through man's unrighteousness? Paul does not even like to write this question down. He says, "I am speaking in human terms."[92] But Paul has heard these questions, and he answers, "May it never be! *(Me genoito!)*" For otherwise, how will God judge the world?"[93] God is God, and we should give thanks. God created us, and He is announcing salvation. He redeemed us, and He sent His Son to die for us. That should be the context in which we ask questions.

Third question, does the gospel of grace say, "Let us do evil that good may come?" – 3:7-8

3:7 *"But if through my lie the truth of God abounded to His glory, why am I also still being judged as a sinner?*
3:8 *And why not say (as we are slanderously reported and as some claim that we say), 'Let us do evil that good may come?' Their condemnation is just."*

If God is glorified, if His righteousness is demonstrated through my sin putting Christ on the cross, then why not just sin? This is

---

92 Romans 3:5
93 Romans 3:6

a common slander of the gospel. Whenever the gospel of grace is fully explained, yesterday or today, whenever we preach and teach the real gospel of God's grace, there will be those who say, well then, we can just sin. There are people in our churches who take the gospel of grace and slander it by saying since God is a God of grace and He forgives sin because of Jesus; it does not matter if we sin. Religionists say, "Well, then we can do anything we want! The more we sin, the more glory to God." Paul does not even waste a *me genoito* on this one. He simply says, "their condemnation is just."[94] Whenever man's sinfulness is exposed, and God's righteousness is exalted, as Paul does in Romans, sinful men will quibble, question and argue.

> **3:9** *"What then? are we better than they? Not at all; for we have already charged that both Jews and Greeks are all under sin."*

Some might ask, just who is this Paul, and who are these Christians to say these things? Paul does not condemn from the standpoint of self-righteousness, and as Christians, we should not either. The gospel of Christ is not us looking down on others. Proclaiming our sinfulness and God's righteousness is not saying we are somehow better. Paul says that all are under sin. There is a bumper sticker in the United States that says, "Christians aren't perfect, just forgiven." That is true.

The verdict – 3:10-18

> **3:10** *"as it is written, 'There is none righteous, not even one;*

---

94 Romans 3:8

3:11 *There is none who understands, There is none who seeks for God,*
3:12 *All have turned aside, together they have become useless; there is none who does good, There is not even one.'*
3:13 *'Their throat is an open grave, With their tongues they keep deceiving,' 'The poison of asps is under their lips;*
3:14 *'Whose mouth is full of cursing and bitterness',*
3:15 *"'Their feet are swift to shed blood,*
3:16 *Destruction and misery are in their paths,*
3:17 *And the path of peace they have not known.'*
3:18 *'There is no fear of God before their eyes.'"*

Beginning in Romans Chapter 1, verse 17, we have seen Paul's fairly lengthy indictment of mankind. Verses 10-18 of Chapter 3 are the verdict. Every verse is a quote from the Old Testament. The verses are a condemnation of the whole human race. All, Jews and Gentiles (Greeks), are under sin Paul writes in verse 9. And then Paul comes to the verdict in verse 10, "as it is written." This settles everything. One day soon the Son will speak to the whole race when God the judge stands up and pronounces the verdict.

Put your name in there – there is none righteous, not even "Scott." There are no exceptions. Have you found the one exception? Are you arrogant enough to say, "Oh, but there are some good people." Sometimes when I share the gospel, people will tell me, "I know a nice person." They tell me about some person that they think is good. When we say that, it betrays our own self-righteousness because if we can find somebody that we think is pretty good, then maybe we are not so bad either. They think, "We should not be condemned." Oh, the arrogance of us saying, "But there are some good people." God looked and He found none. Paul is quoting from Psalm 53:1-3, and it is one of the few Psalms that is repeated.[95]

God is the Divine Physician, the Divine Doctor diagnosing our condition. "Their throat is an open grave, With their tongues they keep deceiving, The poison of asps is under their lips; Whose mouth is full of cursing and bitterness."[96] It is like when you go to the doctor, and he inserts a stick in your mouth to see into your throat. God says, "Their throat is an open grave." The stench! Have you ever smelled dead flesh, an open grave? This is God's appraisal. The Psalmist refers to the throats, tongue, and mouth. Jesus said, what comes out of the mouth comes from the heart.[97] The diagnosis, the verdict, is guilty. What comes out of people's mouths is cursing, bitterness, blasphemy, and deceit. You can hear it on the streets. In verses 15-17, God, the divine historian, says, look at the record of mankind.

I was on an airplane and sat next to a man who is a brilliant surgeon, chairman of the trauma surgery department. As we visited, he told me that he learned his skill during the Vietnam war. He was a very skilled trauma surgeon. He was returning from lecturing in renown medical centers. I asked him about his spiritual life and his relationship with God. He paused and said, "Well, I guess I have to say I'm agnostic." I said, "Why?" He responded, "I've seen so much." In the context of

---

95   Psalms 14 and 53 are almost identical
96   Romans 3:13-14
97   *See* Mathew 15:18

our conversation, I knew that he was referring to all the evil that he had seen in the Vietnam war. Pointing to the luggage rack, he told me that he was reading a book that was helping him to understand life a little bit. I said, "Well, you know as you were telling me about all that you have seen, I was thinking of the book I have read; it's called Romans."

To see the wickedness of man, the bloodshed, and "the path of peace they have not known;"[98] to see man's wickedness is not to indict God. So many people look at man's sinfulness and shake their finger at God. Man does this because of the final verdict in verse 18, perhaps the very worst thing in the whole list, "There is no fear of God before their eyes." This is the indictment. The verdict comes down — guilty on all counts.

The Law closes man's mouth – 3:19-20

> **3:19** *"Now we know that whatever the Law says, it speaks to those who are under the Law, that every mouth may be closed, and all the world may become accountable to God;* **3:20** *Because by the works of the Law no flesh will be justified in His sight; for through the Law comes the knowledge of sin."*

God did not give the Law to justify. No one will stand right before God by keeping religious rules or trying "to turn over a new leaf." The whole race is guilty and without excuse; those who are openly rebellious, like in Romans Chapter 1, and those who are proud and self-confident in their moralism or in their

---

98   Romans 3:17

rituals and religiousness. People ramble on about their philosophies, religions and ways of looking at life, but God's word will silence every mouth.[99]

Paul has done the dirt work. He has excavated man's self-righteousness. He has exposed man's unrighteousness — our sin. Now, beginning in Romans 3:21, he can lay the foundation of Jesus Christ, the Savior.

Study questions

- Why is trust in the Law a false trust (2:17-23)?

- Scripture speaks of circumcision of the heart (see 2:29). What is God asking of us, and how does this differ from reliance on outward rituals?

- Can peoples' unbelief somehow nullify God's word (3:3-4)?

- How would you respond to the claim that there are good people who do not deserve God's judgment?

---

99   *See* Romans 3:19

6

JUSTIFICATION EXPLAINED

Romans 3:21-31

In this section, we have come to the great foundation of our faith. "No man can lay a foundation other than that which is laid, which is Jesus Christ."[100] This is the heart of Romans, the heart of the gospel of God. Paul brought us to this point asking, "How can a just God justify sinners?" That is the great question. We have seen that man is anything but righteous. No amount of self-effort, religion, or morality can make a sinful man right with God. Not even God's holy and righteous Law. "Now we know that whatever the Law says it speaks to those who are under the law that every mouth may be closed and all the world may become accountable to God; because by the works of the Law no flesh will be justified in His sight; for through the Law comes the knowledge of sin."[101] The Law will not and cannot justify. The Law shows us our sinfulness and closes our mouths. And now, in the following verses, God opens His heart.

---

100   1 Corinthians 3:11
101   Romans 3:19-20

Leon Morris, the Australian bible teacher who died in 2006 at the age of 92, taught the Bible for many years in Australia and throughout the world. He waited until late in life to write on Romans, and he said of this paragraph that it is possibly the single most important paragraph ever written. I would agree. If you miss everything else, hear these verses.

"But now ..." — *3:21-22*

3:21 *"But now apart from the Law the righteousness of God has been manifested, being witnessed by the Law and the Prophets,*

3:22 *even the righteousness of God through faith in Jesus Christ for all those who believe; for there is no distinction;"*

"But now..." We turn with relief from looking at man's sinfulness to the heart of God. I mentioned earlier John Mitchell and learning Romans from him. He was Scottish and spoke English with a distinctive accent. I still remember him saying very strongly, "But now...." I remember one day my step-grandfather came for a visit in his old age. They lived far away, so we did not see them very often. My grandfather had come to know Jesus Christ in his 20's while living in Dublin, Ireland. He had a similar distinctive accent. I remember telling him about my joy in Romans, and he said, "Ah, Romans. 'But now...'" I knew he was thinking of this verse, the turning point when you begin to look at the amazing gospel in its purity. "But now apart from the law, the righteousness of God has been manifested."[102] This is the theme of Romans. In the gospel, the righteousness

---

102 Romans 3:21

of God is revealed. We saw this in the theme verse, Romans 1:17, "The righteous man shall live by faith." Paul now begins to unfold the righteousness of God apart from the law. "Even the righteousness of God through faith in Jesus Christ for all those who believe; for there is no distinction."[103] "Whoever will call on the name of the Lord will be saved."[104]

Paul is careful when he speaks to show that he is building on the rest of the Bible. Paul notes at the end of verse 21, "being witnessed by the Law and the Prophets." Paul similarly wrote in the second verse of Romans Chapter 1 that he was "set apart for the gospel of God, which He promised beforehand through His prophets in the Holy Scriptures."[105] Paul started his epistle to the Romans with this point, and he will end there. In his closing doxology, Paul concludes that the gospel and the preaching of Jesus Christ "now is manifested, and by the Scriptures of the prophets, according to the commandment of the eternal God, has been made known to all the nations, leading to obedience of faith."[106] Paul is not saying that he has something different to share; the book of Romans and this gospel is consistent with the whole of Scripture.

Even during his "indictment" in the first two and a half chapters of Romans, Paul quoted or alluded to eleven Old Testament texts. This righteousness of God through faith in Jesus Christ is based on the Old Testament. Faith in Jesus Christ was always what the Bible looked toward. As soon as Adam sinned, God

---

103 Romans 3:22
104 Romans 10:13
105 Romans 1:2
106 Romans 16:26

began to promise a Savior. In Genesis, He mentions the seed of the woman who would bruise his heal as He stomped on the head of the serpent.[107] "Seed of the woman" is an odd way of saying it. We would normally say, "seed of the man." But this is a veiled reference to the virgin birth. Jesus was not tainted by Adam's sin. The Holy Spirit came upon Mary and so we have "Immanuel, God with us."[108]

Paul underlines, "even the righteousness of God through faith in Jesus Christ."[109] In these verses, Paul further explains verse 17 of Romans Chapter 1. That is why earlier I commented that the righteousness of God speaks not only of His righteousness but that He declares righteous those who put their faith in Christ. The book of Romans is always referring to how we can be righteous through faith in Christ. Many people miss that. Martin Luther, as was mentioned, said he hated that phrase because it only further condemned him when he thought of it as only the righteousness of God. But as he was studying Romans and saw that it is referring to the fact that a righteous God can declare a sinner righteous, it set him free.

For all have sinned – 3:23

3:23 *"for all have sinned and fall short of the glory of God,"*

The essence of sin is falling short of God's glory. We have very little idea how sinful sin really is. We tend to think in terms of

---

107   Genesis 3:15
108   *See* Matthew 1:23
109   Romans 3:22

gradation of sin; some sin, more sin, bad sin, lesser sin. But all sin absolutely separates us from the glory of God. We have fallen short, infinitely short, of what we were meant to be and what we should be. We fall short of the glory of God. Verse 23 is a succinct summary of all that Paul has said in Romans. All are equally sinful. All equally fall short. No one comes even close to God's glory.

A few years back, I had the opportunity to visit Ethiopia, where I gave a series of messages on Romans as part of the Romans Project. I was in Addis Ababa, the highest city in Africa and one of the highest capitals in the world. The first day there, I was able to go up to Entoto Hill, where we prayed. At 3200 meters, it is the highest point in the city. But even at such a high elevation, does anyone believe that they can somehow jump and touch the glory of God? Are you really any closer to God? The heavens are telling of the glory of God.[110] Scientists measure the heavens in statistics we cannot even grasp. But one thing is certain, whether we are at sea level or the highest point in Addis Ababa, we cannot reach the stars. God says, "all have sinned and fall short of the glory of God."[111]

Romans 3:24-26

3:24 *"being justified as a gift by His grace through the redemption which is in Christ Jesus;*
3:25 *whom God displayed publicly as a propitiation in His blood through faith. This was to demonstrate His*

---

110   Psalm 19:1
111   Romans 3:23

righteousness, because in the forbearance of God He passed over the sins previously committed;
3:26 *for the demonstration, I say, of His righteousness at the present time, that He would be just and the justifier of the one who has faith in Jesus."*

Being justified as a gift – without cost

Paul then writes, "being justified as a gift by His grace through the redemption which is in Christ Jesus."[112] Justified, declared right, is the verb form of the term "righteousness." So, I ask the question, "How can a righteous God justify a sinner?" It is helpful to rephrase the question and ask, "How can a just God justify a sinner?" Or, "How can a righteous God "righteousfy" a sinner? "Righteousfy" is not an actual word in English, but it helps us to understand the meaning of this verse. This great matter of justification is about a righteous God declaring sinners righteous.

"Being justified as a gift." The Greek word behind "gift" is "*dóron*." This is translated elsewhere in the New Testament as "freely." "Freely you received, freely give."[113] It is only used nine times in the New Testament and it speaks of "without charge," "without cost." "For the wages of sin is death, but the free gift of God is eternal life in Christ Jesus our Lord."[114] The Bible closes with this truth in Revelation. "And He said to me, 'It is done. I am the Alpha and the Omega, the beginning and

---

112 Romans 3:24
113 Matthew 10:8
114 Romans 6:23

the end. I will give to the one who thirsts from the spring of the water of life without cost.'"[115] I will give "without cost" — *dóron.* Later it is written, "The Spirit and the bride say, 'Come.' … And let the one who is thirsty come; let the one who wishes take the water of life without cost."[116]

The Gospel of John uses this term, *dóron,* in a wholly different connection. In John 15, Jesus is telling his disciples, the world will hate you; it hated me. Do not expect the slave will get better treatment than the master. Jesus then explains, "But they have done this in order that the word may be fulfilled that is written in their Law, 'They hated Me without a cause.'"[117] Jesus is quoting Psalm 69:4, "Those who hate me without a cause *(dóron)*." There was no reason to hate Jesus. He went about doing good and healing and helping. He spoke like no man ever spoke. They hated Him for no reason — without a cause.

We have nothing to offer Him. We cannot pay for our salvation. We pull out our righteousness and He says it is "a filthy garment."[118] But praise God, He justifies freely, without cost – *dóron.* There is nothing in me that deserves to be saved. I am without excuse. "But now apart from the Law the righteousness of God has been manifested … being justified as a gift *(dóron)*."[119] Do not look for anything in yourself that is worth saving or that somehow merits God's favor. Christ Jesus came into the world to save sinners.

---

115 Revelation 21:6
116 Revelation 22:17
117 John 15:25
118 Isaiah 64:6
119 Romans 3:21 and 24

Redemption which is in Christ Jesus

Justification is free, but at the same time, it is very costly. Verse 24 continues, "through the redemption which is in Christ Jesus." God purchased us with His Son's blood; redemption. He gives us freely that which cost Him everything. Peter writes we were "not redeemed with perishable things like silver or gold … but with precious blood, as of a lamb unblemished and spotless, the blood of Christ."[120] God paid infinitely for our salvation. Grace is never cheap. It is infinitely expensive. God uses this language to help us see what He did to redeem us from the slavery of sin. He paid it all! He paid not with all the money in the world but by the blood of His beloved Son.

This is why it is such an insult to try to believe that there are other ways to God. If there were another way to God, He would never have sent his Son. If we could just keep some rules, He would have said, "Keep them!" People say, "Well, you have your religion, we have ours. All religions pretty much say the same thing. All roads lead to the top of the mountain." That is an insult to the blood of Jesus Christ. Now I speak reverently when I say this, if there were any other way to be right with God than through Jesus Christ, then God made a terrible mistake when he gave his Son. I really do not like to say that, but I say it because the Bible says it. In Galatians, Paul is arguing the same great doctrine of justification by faith in Jesus Christ. "I do not nullify the grace of God, for if righteousness comes through the Law, then Christ died needlessly."[121] But Christ

---

120 1 Peter 1:18-19
121 Galatians 2:21

JUSTIFICATION EXPLAINED · **77**

did not die needlessly. Righteousness does not come through the Law.

> *"Nevertheless knowing that a man is not justified by the works of the Law but through faith in Christ Jesus, even we have believed in Christ Jesus, so that we may be justified by faith in Christ and not by the works of the Law; since by the works of the Law shall no flesh be justified."*[122]

Redemption of a soul is costly. It was freely offered to us, but it cost God everything. He moved heaven and earth to save us. He did more than that, He sent his Son to a sinful world to become sin on the cross for us.

Always when we proclaim the gospel, we have to keep these two truths woven together as the Bible does. We are justified as a gift *(dóron)* by grace, through the redemption, which is in Christ Jesus — the blood of Christ. The blood of bulls and goats could not take away sin. All the Old Testament sacrifices could never take away sin. They all pointed ahead to the Lamb of God. The book of Hebrews argues this point.

> *"For the Law, since it has only a shadow of the good things to come and not the very form of things, can never, by the same sacrifices which they offer continually year by year, make perfect those who draw near. Otherwise, would they not have ceased to be offered, because the worshipers, having once been cleansed,*

122 Galatians 2:16

would no longer have had consciousness of sins? But in
those sacrifices there is a reminder of sins year by year.
For it is impossible for the blood of bulls and goats to
take away sins."[123]

Hebrews Chapter 10 talks about preparing a body for His Son to
come and do His will and that He would offer His life a ransom
for us. "Sacrifices and offerings and whole burnt offerings…
You have not desired."[124] Jesus said through the Psalmist, "I
have come to do Your will."[125] Jesus offered His life, and by
His will, we have been sanctified through the offering of the
body of Jesus Christ once for all. "Every priest stands daily
ministering and offering time after time the same sacrifices,
which can never take away sins; but He, having offered one
sacrifice for sins for all time, sat down at the right hand of
God."[126] Our redemption is costly. Jesus Christ offered His
life and shed His blood for you and for me. The argument
in Hebrews, these two great themes — free and costly, are
imbedded in Romans 3:24.

A propitiation in His blood

"The redemption, which is in Christ Jesus," Paul continues,
"whom God displayed publicly as a propitiation in His blood
through faith." This is the great answer to the question asked
above, "How can God, a righteous God, declare a sinful man
right?" Jesus was our propitiation (our atonement). God

---

123 Hebrews 10:1-4
124 Hebrews 10:8
125 Hebrews 10:9
126 Hebrews 10:11-12

displayed Him publicly as a propitiation in His blood. The Old Testament sacrificial system taught the need for a blood sacrifice. The book of Hebrews says without the shedding of blood, there is no forgiveness. But it also says, all those sacrifices did not propitiate. God's wrath against sin is real. "The wages of sin is death."[127] "For in the day that you eat from [that tree] you will surely die."[128] Someone had to die. Jesus Christ, the righteous, bore our sins in His body, and He propitiated (appeased) God so that God is free to be merciful to you and me.

The first half of verse 25 talks about the blood of the cross that we lay hold of by faith. It is not our faith that saves us; it is the object of our faith that saves. This propitiation demonstrated His righteousness because, in the forbearance of God, He passed over the sins previously committed. In the Old Testament, they sinned as we sin. God passed over their sins looking ahead to the cross. A believer would be saved by looking ahead, as we are saved by looking back. The cross is the great public demonstration that God is righteous, and that sin must be paid for. God cannot overlook sin. And yet He did overlook sin because of the cross. Whenever we teach the Bible, wherever we are at, we should always focus on God's focus; His beloved Son and what He did on the cross. How can God be just and justify sinners? — the cross of Jesus Christ.

Looking at the last phrase in verse 26, who is justified? The one who goes to church? May it never be. The one who is baptized?

---

127 Romans 6:23
128 Genesis 2:17

The one who keeps the Law? No. He is justified "who has faith in Jesus." Our faith is not in the church or Christianity. Our faith is in Jesus. We are justified!

Where then is boasting? – 3:27-31

> **3:27** *"Where then is boasting? It is excluded. By what kind of law? Of works? No, but by a law of faith.*
>
> **3:28** *For we maintain that a man is justified by faith apart from works of the Law.*
>
> **3:29** *Or is God the God of Jews only? Is He not the God of Gentiles also? Yes, of Gentiles also,*
>
> **3:30** *if indeed God is one – and He will justify the circumcised by faith and the uncircumcised through faith.*
>
> **3:31** *Do we then nullify the Law through faith? May it never be! On the contrary, we establish the Law."*

Paul then asks, "Where then is boasting?"[129] The gospel of grace, the gospel of God, the gospel of Romans excludes boasting. On what kind of principle is there a basis for boasting? By works? No, but by a law of faith. There is no merit in faith alone. Faith is laying hold of God's grace. Just think of how ugly heaven would be if we earned it. It would be full of boasting! Heaven would not be heaven if boasting were not excluded. How are we justified? By the blood of Jesus Christ. I have nothing to claim but that God's Son died for me and rose again on my behalf. Boasting is excluded.

---

129 Romans 3:27

Is God's justification for the Jews only? "Is God the God of the Jews only? Is he not the God of Gentiles also? Yes, of Gentiles also, if indeed God is one."[130] The gospel is not only for Israel, or America, or Africa. He is God of both the "Jew' and "Gentile;" that covers everybody. God will "justify the circumcised by faith and the uncircumcised through faith."[131]

Does the gospel that Paul is teaching contradict the Old Testament? Do we then nullify the Law through faith? *Me genoito.* "On the contrary we establish the Law."[132] What did the Law say? The day you eat of that tree, you would surely die! "The wages of sin is death."[133] "The soul that sins will die."[134] Someone had to die. Jesus Christ, the righteous, died in our place. This is the gospel!

---

130   Romans 3:29-30
131   Romans 3:30
132   Romans 3:31
133   Romans 6:23
134   Ezekiel 18:4

Study questions

- Verse 3:21 begins, "But now ... " Why should believers rejoice in those words? How does this mark a turning point in Paul's letter to the Romans?

- What is the significance of "being justified as a gift" (3:24)?

- Why was it necessary for Christ to be a "propitiation in His blood" for us (3:25)?

- What are some of the ways people try to boast of their own righteousness? Why is all such boasting excluded (3:27)?

7

JUSTIFICATION ILLUSTRATED

Romans 4

We saw in Romans Chapter 3 one of the clearest explanations in the Bible of the doctrine of justification. It is accomplished apart from the Law through faith in Christ Jesus.[135] All of us have fallen short of God's glory. We are justified freely, without any cost to ourselves, "through the redemption which is in Christ Jesus."[136] The Law said, and the Bible teaches, that sin brings death. The gospel proclaims that Christ conquered sin and death by rising from the dead. Here in Chapter 4, we see this great doctrine of justification illustrated. Paul has been preaching for a long time. He knows the kinds of questions that arise when you proclaim the gospel, and he raises them here.

What about Abraham? – 4:1-3

4:1 *"What then shall we say that Abraham, our forefather according to the flesh, has found?*

---

135   Romans 3:21-22
136   Romans 3:23-24

4:2 *For if Abraham was justified by works, he has something to boast about; but not before God.*
4:3 *For what does the Scripture say? "And Abraham believed God, and it was reckoned to him as righteousness."*

"What about Abraham?" the Jews would say. Many people today think we are saved by grace today in the New Testament, but in the Old Testament they were saved by the Law. And they will raise this question, "What about Abraham?" Abraham stands tall in the Scripture; he still stands tall in our world. The Jews revered Abraham. Islam claims Abraham. As Christians, he is the father of all who believe; all who exercise faith in Jesus Christ. So, we want to pay close attention to what Paul says about him. "If Abraham was justified by works, he has something to boast about, but not before God." Paul already said in Romans Chapter 3, there is no boasting in our works.

At the start of verse 3, Paul asks once again, "What does the Scripture say?" That should always be the question. Not, what this man, or that church, or this Christian movement says. Rather, what does the Scripture say? We should habitually ask ourselves, "What does the Bible say on every question of life?" And surely on this question of justification, we should ask, "What does the Scripture say?" "Abraham believed God, and it was reckoned to him as righteousness."[137] People have always been saved by faith. In every era, salvation is by grace through faith, in the Old and New Testaments. Abraham was justified by faith; he believed God. Abraham took God at His word, and he was reckoned as righteousness.

---

137 Romans 4:3, quoting Genesis 15:6

Justification defined

It is good to let the Bible define its own terms. To many people, words like justification or sanctification are just big words. We ask ourselves, what does justification mean? Paul has been explaining the doctrine of justification. Abraham was not "justified by works," but "he believed God." And then, rather than saying "he was justified," Paul uses the phrase, "it was reckoned to him as righteousness." There you have the definition of justification. It means to have the righteousness of God credited to your account. In 2 Corinthians, Paul puts it this way: "He made Him who knew no sin to be sin on our behalf, so that we might become the righteousness of God in Him."[138] This is the great exchange! Christ's righteousness is charged to our account.

Justification is apart from works – 4:4-5

4:4 *"Now to the one who works, his wage is not reckoned as a favor but as what is due.*

4:5 *But to the one who does not work, but believes in Him who justifies the ungodly, his faith is reckoned as righteousness,"*

In verses 4 and 5, Paul gives another illustration of justification. If we understand what he is saying, it will shock us. In life, you work and you receive a wage. Paul says that is the way it is in verse 4. In contrast, as he talks about our justification in verse 5, he says we do not work. We "believe in Him who justifies the ungodly" and "faith is reckoned (counted) as righteousness" to

138   2 Corinthians 5:21

us.[139] This is one of the best statements of grace in the Bible. These two verses often set people free in understanding the doctrine of justification.

I walked up to a man years ago on a university campus during the post-Vietnam era. He had been a soldier in the Vietnam War. He was still very rough-looking. He had done things in the war that he was not proud of. As I tried to talk to him about Jesus, it was hard to overcome his exterior roughness. He still had on his camouflage fatigues, and he just looked hard. But as I began to explain the gospel, he started to listen. He had been raised in a church where he had been told that you must be good to be right with God. He was like many people who heard about Christianity on the fringe but had never really understood the gospel. As I got the Bible out, I read to him Romans 4:4 -5, and he looked at me and said, "What kind of Bible is that?" And I said, "It's just a Bible." And he said, "Let me see that," and he took it and he read it. "Now to the one who works, his wage is not reckoned as a favor but as what is due. But to the one who does not work, but believes in Him who justifies the ungodly, his faith is reckoned as righteousness." My friend was ungodly, but as he read this, I watched him grasp the good news. He could be declared righteous. He could be right with God. I had the joy of watching as he prayed and asked Jesus to forgive him, and he was declared righteous. I believe these two verses should be read often in evangelism — they get at the core of the gospel. If they are understood, they shock you. My friend was born again, and he

139 Romans 4:5

grew, and his wife became a Christian. It was a beautiful thing to see the transformation of the gospel in his life.

Years later, a prominent businessman was coming to my church. He was the CEO (head) of the company, and he was interested in what I was preaching. He had me over to his house. He had been financially successful, and we sat in the backyard where he had a swimming pool. As I was explaining the gospel, he was listening and interested. At one point, I got the Bible out and I read him verses 4 and 5. He understood verse 4; "to the one who works, his wage is not reckoned as a favor, but as what is due." But when I read him verse 5, he said to me, "What kind of Bible are you reading?" Just like my other friend had asked, and I said, "Just a Bible." He said, "Read it again." (He was the head of the company and was used to telling people what to do). I read it again, and he said, "You misread that." I said, "No, I didn't." He understood it, but he could not believe it. That is not the way life works. He was a businessman; you work, you gain, you earn. He could not accept that God would give something freely. He continued to listen, but I regret to tell you he would not believe. He still came to church for a while, and he would listen. He went on a big game hunting trip in Canada, and he had a heart attack and died. As far as I know, he never believed in the Lord Jesus Christ. Those memories are fresh in my heart still because both men understood. One received and one rejected. Verses 4 and 5 help people understand how we are justified; how we have had the righteousness of God credited to our account.

Justification includes forgiveness – 4:6-8

4:6 *"just as David also speaks of the blessing upon the man to whom God reckons righteousness apart from works:*
4:7 *'Blessed are those whose lawless deeds have been forgiven, and whose sins have been covered.*
4:8 *Blessed is the man whose sin the Lord will not take into account.'"*

If there is someone who would rival Abraham in Old Testament prominence, it is David. David was justified (saved) the same way that Abraham was, the same way anyone is saved — by grace through faith. David had sinned greatly. David spoke in the 32nd Psalm, "How blessed is he whose sins have been covered, whose lawless deeds have been forgiven."[140] David took another man's wife. He took the wife of his dear and loyal friend Uriah. Then he tried to cover it up by murdering Uriah. When the gravity of his sin hit him, he confessed, "Against You, You only, I have sinned."[141] He knew the weight of guilt. If ever a man sinned against another man, it was David. He had betrayed Uriah, one of his mighty men. But when the real gravity of sin hit him, he knew it was against God that he had sinned, and when God forgave him, he rejoiced.

Justification includes forgiveness, praise God, but it is not limited to forgiveness. If I were just declared innocent, I would be guilty again before tonight's meal. It is more than mere forgiveness. I do not say that lightly because I am so glad for my forgiveness. When you come to Christ, you are forgiven.

---

140 Psalms 32:1
141 Psalms 51:4

The moment you come to Christ, there is a removal and a bestowal. Every Christian, whether you just became a Christian or you have been a Christian for decades, the moment you put your faith in Christ, there is a removal of sin and a bestowal of the Holy Spirit. When I came to know Christ, I wanted to be forgiven. I find that to be precious to all our hearts to know that our sins have been forgiven. But again, justification is more than mere forgiveness. If I came to Christ and were only forgiven, I would be vulnerable again to sinning. This is not to minimize forgiveness. But justification is being declared righteous. In the great courtroom drama that Paul has been laying out, the indictment has been called out; I am without excuse. But Christ stood in my place. The theologians speak of it as "substitutionary atonement." Because of what Christ did, I am declared righteous.

Justification is apart from Religious ritual – 4:9-12

Paul has previously explained that justification is based on the cross.[142] It excludes any kind of boasting or merit.[143] It is apart from works[144] and includes forgiveness.[145] Now, in verses 9-12, he writes that justification is apart from any kind of religious ritual or rite. Although he is specifically writing about circumcision, this can be applied to baptism and other kinds of rituals that God has given but which have nothing to do with our justification.

142   Romans 3:21-26
143   Romans 3:27 — 4:3
144   Romans 4:4-5
145   Romans 4:6-8

4:9 *"Is this blessing then upon the circumcised, or upon the uncircumcised also? For we say, 'Faith was reckoned to Abraham as righteousness.'*
4:10 *How then was it reckoned? While he was circumcised, or uncircumcised? Not while circumcised, but uncircumcised;*
4:11 *and he received the sign of circumcision, a seal of the righteousness of the faith which he had while uncircumcised, that he might be the father of all who believe without being circumcised, that righteousness might be reckoned to them,*
4:12 *and the father of circumcision to those who not only are of the circumcision, but who also follow in the steps of the faith of our father Abraham which he had while uncircumcised."*

Paul asks the question in verse 10, "How was this righteousness reckoned to Abraham? While he was circumcised or uncircumcised?" This is a crucial question. It is asked practically in Acts 16, where the jailer cried out, "What must I do to be saved?"[146] The response: "Believe in the Lord Jesus, and you will be saved."[147] Asked theologically, it could be phrased this way, "Is the cross of Christ enough?" How was Abraham justified? While circumcised or uncircumcised?

We do not know exactly how old Abraham was when he believed God and was declared righteous in Genesis 15. We know he was 75 years old when God called him to the promised

---

146 Acts 16:30
147 Acts 16:31

land in Genesis 12. We know later in Chapter 16 of Genesis, Sarah was unable to conceive, and she told Abraham to take Hagar, and Ishmael was born. In Genesis 17, when Ishmael was 13 years old, and Abraham was 99, the rite of circumcision was given.[148] This was long after Abraham had been justified. So, Paul answers the question of how Abraham was justified with the statement, "Not while circumcised, but uncircumcised."

Justification is through Jesus Christ. So, what must I do to be saved? Some churches say, you need to believe in Jesus and His cross, but you also must be circumcised; you must be baptized; you must keep the Ten Commandments. There are many ways to add to the cross. That is the situation Paul is addressing in the book of Galatians where he says, if anyone "should preach to you a different gospel contrary to what we have preached to you, he is to be accursed!"[149] When you add to the cross, you subtract from the cross; you disdain the finished work of Christ. Jesus said, "It is finished!"[150] The great proof of this is that He rose from the dead. Abraham believed God, and it was reckoned to him as righteousness, apart from any ritual or rite such as circumcision.

Justification is apart from the Law – 4:13-16

4:13 *"For the promise to Abraham or to his descendants that he would be heir of the world was not through the Law, but through the righteousness of faith.*

---

148 Genesis 17:11-12
149 Galatians 1:8
150 John 19:30

> **4:14** *For if those who are of the Law are heirs, faith is made void and the promise is nullified;*
> **4:15** *for the Law brings about wrath, but where there is no law, neither is there violation.*
> **4:16** *For this reason it is by faith, that it might be in accordance with grace, in order that the promise may be certain to all the descendants, not only to those who are of the Law, but also to those who are of the faith of Abraham, who is the father of us all."*

Paul reiterates that justification is apart from the Law in verses 13 through 16. "If those who are of the Law are heirs, faith is made void and the promise is nullified."[151] You cannot mix Law and grace. Paul writes later in Romans Chapter 11, "If it is by grace, it is no longer on the basis of works, otherwise grace is no longer grace."[152] You cannot put God in your debt. You cannot put God in a position where He owes you something. All attempts to earn salvation are to misunderstand grace.

The illustration of justification in Abraham's life teaches us not to nullify grace. Do not make the cross of Christ void. The reason our justification is certain is that it is based on the work of another — Jesus Christ, the Righteous One. "For this reason it is by faith, that it might be in accordance with grace, in order that the promise may be certain to all the descendants."[153] God's promise is certain, guaranteed, to all who have been justified by the finished work of the cross.

---

151 Romans 4:14
152 Romans 11:6
153 Romans 4:16

Abraham was Justified by faith in the God of Resurrection – 4:17-25

4:17 *"(as it is written, 'A father of many nations have I made you') in the sight of Him who he believed, even God, who gives life to the dead and calls into being that which does not exist.*

4:18 *In hope against hope he believed, in order that he might become a father of many nations, according to that which had been spoken, 'So shall your descendants be.'*

4:19 *And without becoming weak in faith he contemplated his own body, now as good as dead since he was about a hundred years old, and the deadness of Sarah's womb;*

4:20 *yet, with respect to the promise of God, he did not waiver in unbelief, but grew strong in faith, giving glory to God,*

4:21 *and being fully assured that what He had promised, He was able also to perform.*

4:22 *Therefore also it was reckoned to him as righteousness.*

4:23 *Now not for his sake only was it written, that 'it was reckoned to him,'*

4:24 *but for our sake also, to whom it will be reckoned, as those who believe in Him who raised Jesus our Lord from the dead,*

4:25 *He who was delivered up because of our transgressions, and was raised because of our justification."*

Abraham did not merely believe that God exists, he believed that God is the God of resurrection "who gives life to the dead."[154]

---

154 Romans 4:17

God said, I will make you the "father of many nations,"[155] and I am going to give you a son.[156] Abraham was tempted to think that this could be Ishmael. But no, through Sarah he would have a son. Abraham looked at his circumstances; he was almost a hundred years old and Sarah was barren. "Yet, with respect to the promise of God, he did not waiver in unbelief but grew strong in faith, giving glory to God."[157] Abraham took God at His word. We know who the real son of Abraham is. Our Lord Jesus Christ came through the line of Isaac. Abraham took God at His word regarding his son, and he was reckoned righteous.

Taking God at His word gives glory to God. We glorify God when we believe His Word, even when the circumstances do not look like it will work out. Abraham was fully assured that God was able to perform what had been promised to him. Hebrews says, "Abraham considered that God is able to raise people from the dead."[158] Later Abraham was tested by being instructed to offer up his son. This was yet another beautiful picture of the Father offering up his Son for us.

This was written not merely for Abraham but for all who follow in Abraham's footsteps. God pre-wrote the story of Abraham and recorded it for us who have been justified just like Abraham was, taking God at His word regarding his Son. "Not for his sake only was it written, that 'it was reckoned to him,' but

---

155 *Id.,* quoting Genesis 17:5
156 Genesis 15:3-4
157 Romans 4:20
158 Hebrew 11:19

for our sake also, to whom it will be reckoned, as those who believe in Him who raised Jesus our Lord from the dead."[159]

In Romans Chapter 3, Paul describes a Christian as one who has faith in Jesus. Here, Paul further explains that Christians "believe in Him who raised Jesus our Lord from the dead." Justification is through faith in the God of resurrection. When we talk about the "word of the cross," we are speaking of the death, burial and resurrection of the Lord Jesus Christ.

Paul concludes by describing our Lord as "He who was delivered up because of our transgressions."[160] He was delivered up to the cross because of our sin, "and He was raised because of our justification."[161] When a person becomes a Christian, they not only believe that this happened in history, but the Holy Spirit personally applies it to us. It was my sin that He died for. It was my justification that He rose for. This is a personal faith in a personal Savior who died for me and was raised on my behalf.

---

159 Romans 4:23-24
160 Romans 4:25
161 *Id.*

Study questions

- Describe what it means to be "justified."

- Paul gives the example of David in verses 4:6-8. What does David's example say about what it means to be made righteous or justified?

- Why does Paul ask whether Abraham was credited with righteousness while circumcised or uncircumcised (4:9-12)? What does the answer to that question tell us about what we must do to be saved?

- Jews consider Abraham to be their father. In what way is Abraham "the father of us all" (4:16)?

8

THE PERMANENCE OF JUSTIFICATION

Romans Chapter 5

We have been looking at this great matter of justification. To be justified is to be declared righteous; to have Christ's righteousness charged to our account. In one sense, from verse 1 of Romans until now, Paul has been driving home one main point: the basis of a sinner's standing before God rests not in himself but in another – Jesus Christ.

In Paul's letter to the Romans and throughout the New Testament, he uses the phrase: "in Christ." The great doctrine of justification is the basis of my standing "in Christ." This will tie into our identification with Christ discussed in Romans Chapter 6 and following, which theologically we speak of as "sanctification." But here in Romans Chapter 5, Paul is still talking about justification, and because our standing is grounded in another's righteousness, Christ Jesus, our justification is absolutely secure!

Paul has emphasized justification by faith. But as he has explained it, we recognize that it is not faith that justifies. Rather, it is the object of our faith: the finished work of Jesus Christ — His death, burial, and resurrection. Romans Chapter 5 gives three lines of arguments, three lines of truth, for why our justification is permanent. First, faith is not destroyed by troubles or trials but strengthened. Second, God's great love demonstrated at the cross. And third, the parallel between Adam and Christ; what is sometimes referred to as "representative justification."

Faith is not destroyed by troubles – 5:1-5

In verses 1 through 5, Paul argues that we can never lose our right standing before God because our faith is not destroyed by trouble or trials but rather strengthened.

> **5:1** *"Therefore having been justified by faith, we have peace with God through our Lord Jesus Christ,*
> **5:2** *through whom also we have obtained our introduction by faith into this grace in which we stand; and we exult in hope of the glory of God.*
> **5:3** *And not only this, but we also exult in our tribulations, knowing that tribulation brings about perseverance;*
> **5:4** *and perseverance, proven character; and proven character, hope;*
> **5:5** *and hope does not disappoint, because the Love of God has been poured out within our hearts through the Holy Spirit who was given to us."*

Paul always links his thoughts together. Romans is logical and persuasive in that way. Often the link he uses is the first word of verse one, "therefore." "Therefore having been justified by faith, we have peace with God through our Lord Jesus Christ."[162] In a world of unrest and lack of peace, we have peace. We speak of all kinds of peace: international peace, personal peace, circumstantial peace, peace with our creator. Paul is speaking of "the peace of God, which surpasses all comprehension" when we cast our anxieties on Him.[163] We have experiential peace as we walk with the Lord. Jesus said, "In the world you have tribulation, but take courage; I have overcome the world." "These things I have spoken to you, so that in Me you may have peace."[164] Jesus spoke of many varieties of peace, peace at home, peace within your marriage, inner peace. All these are possible only because "we have peace with God."

Paul also writes of our salvation in these first two verses — past, present, and future. In the past – "having been justified by faith." In the present – "we have peace with God." And in the future – "we exult in hope of the glory of God."[165] We look forward to His return. Paul said earlier there is no boasting, but we can boast in God and in our hope in Him in the future.

Then Paul says,
> *"And not only this, but we also exult in our tribulations, knowing that tribulation brings about perseverance; and perseverance, proven character; and proven character,*

---

162 Romans 5:1
163 Philippians 4:7
164 John 16:33
165 Romans 5:2

hope; and hope does not disappoint, because the Love of God has been poured out within our hearts through the Holy Spirit who was given to us."[166]

If I am justified by faith, I might fear what if my faith falters? But Paul teaches that true faith is never destroyed by trouble; it is strengthened. James says the same thing; we "consider it all joy ... when [we] encounter various trials, knowing that the testing of [our] faith produces endurance."[167] God uses trouble in our lives not to destroy our faith or undermine it but to strengthen our faith and build it.

This chain of character building that God does in our life is a beautiful chain of consequence. Biblically, hope is absolutely certain. Faith is looking back to the cross, and hope is faith looking ahead. In one sense they are very similar concepts, and our hope is absolutely certain because of the object of our hope: Jesus Christ.

"This hope we have as an anchor of the soul, a hope both sure and steadfast and one which enters within the veil, where Jesus has entered as a forerunner for us, having become a high priest forever according to the order of Melchizedek."[168]

Jesus rose from the dead; He ascended into heaven; He is seated at the Right Hand of God; He is within the veil; He is

---

166 Romans 5:3-5
167 James 1:2
168 Hebrews 6:19-20

in the Holy of Holies, and He is our forerunner. Our hope is absolutely certain. Whatever trials we go through, whatever God allows us to go through, it will not destroy our faith — our hope. It will strengthen our faith and hope. If you have been a Christian for any length of time, you have seen believers who have gone through real trials, and they come out stronger. That is the work of God's grace in our lives.

After Paul mentions hope in verse 5, he says, "and hope does not disappoint, because the love of God has been poured out within our hearts through the Holy Spirit who was given to us."[169] We became conscious of God's great love for us through the ministry of the Holy Spirit. He opened our blinded eyes to the great love at the cross. This is the first mention of the word "love" in Romans. Surprisingly, it is also the first mention of the Holy Spirit, other than a brief reference in Chapter 1, verse 4, that Christ was raised from the dead through the Holy Spirit. Jesus said when the Holy Spirit comes, He "will convict the world concerning sin, and righteousness, and judgment."[170] The Holy Spirit initially brought me to Christ. He bears witness with my spirit that I am a child of God. We will see in Romans Chapter 8 that the Holy Spirit teaches us and guides us. But for now, Paul mentions Him as the one who opened us up to the love of God.

---

169   Romans 5:5
170   John 16:8

God's great love demonstrated at the Cross – 5:6-11

In the following verses, Paul gives us the great objective statement of God's love. Our justification is secure and cannot be lost because of God's great love demonstrated at the cross.

> **5:6** *"For while we were still helpless, at the right time Christ died for the ungodly.*
> **5:7** *For one will hardly die for a righteous man; though perhaps for the good man someone would dare even to die.*
> **5:8** *But God demonstrates His own love toward us, in that while we were yet sinners, Christ died for us.*
> **5:9** *Much more then, having now been justified by His blood, we shall be saved from the wrath of God through Him.*
> **5:10** *For if while we were enemies, we were reconciled to God through the death of His Son, much more, having been reconciled, we shall be saved by His life.*
> **5:11** *And not only this, but we also exult in God through our Lord Jesus Christ through whom we have now received the reconciliation."*

Paul describes the love of God as a "much more" love. If God loved me when I was his enemy, "much more" He loves me now that I am His child. Paul gives the argument of the paragraph in verse 9, "Much more then, having been justified by His blood, we shall be saved from the wrath of God through Him." God did the harder thing — He gave his Son for sinners. He will now do the lesser, the easier thing – He will keep secure those of us who have been purchased by the blood of his Son.

There are four keywords in verses 6-10: "helpless," "ungodly," "sinners," and "enemies." "For while we were still <u>helpless</u>, at the right time Christ died for the <u>ungodly</u>."[171] "While we were yet <u>sinners</u>, Christ died for us."[172] And "For if while we were <u>enemies</u>, we were reconciled."[173] I was a helpless, ungodly sinner who was an enemy of God. That is who Christ died for. I was helpless with no ability to help God. Sometimes people say, "God helps those who help themselves." They speak of salvation that way, "You have to do your part, and then He will do His part." I have heard people quote it like it were scripture, but you will not find it in the Bible. God helps the helpless! We must come to Him as helpless. The second word, "ungodly," speaks of those with no inclination towards God. "Sinners" – we are sinners by nature, by practice, by habit. And finally, "enemies" – we are hostile rebels. That is who Christ died for. These words are helpful when we are trying to explain justification and help believers know that their justification is secure. If God loved me when I was a helpless, ungodly sinner and enemy, "much more" does He love me now that I have been justified.

The question is often asked, can a believer lose his salvation? Probably every believer worries about that at one point in time. I ask some of the following questions of people who think they could lose their salvation. "What were you when you were saved? What were you when Christ died for you?" And if they do not know, I will help them with these verses and give them

---

171   Romans 5:6
172   Romans 5:8
173   Romans 5:10

the above fourfold description. Who saved you? Christ. How did He save you? He died for your sins. How many of them? All of them. God said He took all our transgressions and nailed them at the cross. So, what are you worried about? Well sin; failure. I say again, "Who did Christ die for? Sinners. Why did He come? To save sinners." But what if my faith fails? Paul just explained that faith is strengthened by troubles. Christ did not die for the faithful ones, He died for the <u>helpless</u>, <u>ungodly sinner</u> who is an <u>enemy</u> of God. I say all this to focus our attention away from ourselves and on to the cross and what God has done for us. "God demonstrates His own love toward us, in that while we were yet sinners, Christ died for us."[174] This is the great statement of His love — the cross.

Almost invariably, when God speaks of His love for us, it is in the past tense. "For God so loved the world, that He gave His only begotten Son."[175] That is <u>not</u> to say, God used to love us. When God speaks of His love, He uses the past tense because He is pointing us back to the great demonstration of His love. How do I know God loves me? He sent his Son to die for me. How do I know that His love will not change? Jesus died for me when I was a sinner, when I was an enemy, when I was a rebel. He constantly points us back to the cross. "In this is love, not that we loved God, but that He loved us and sent His Son to be the propitiation for our sins."[176] We need to enjoy and bask in that love. The great demonstration of His love is that He gave his only Son. Our justification is permanent because

---

174   Romans 5:8
175   John 3:16
176   1 John 4:10

God loved us at the cross and declared us righteous. Now that we are His children, we are experiencing a "much more" love.

Lastly, pay attention to the phrase in verse 11, "through our Lord Jesus Christ." Paul will use that phrase and a similar one, "in Christ," again and again in the next few chapters of Romans. It reiterates that our standing before God is on the merit of another, "through our Lord Jesus Christ." "For the wages of sin is death, but the free gift of God is eternal life in Christ Jesus our Lord."[177]

The parallel between Adam and Christ – 5:12-21

Paul's final argument is that the security of our justification is based on the analogy between Adam and Christ. This passage argues this as strongly as anywhere in the Bible. It was described earlier as "representative justification." Adam was the head of a race. Adam sinned and brought condemnation to the whole race. Christ is the head of the new race, and His one act of justification is imputed to everyone in the new race.

> **5:12** *"Therefore, just as through one man sin entered into the world, and death through sin, and so death spread to all men, because all sinned –*
> **5:13** *for until the Law sin was in the world; but sin is not imputed when there is no law.*

---

177   Romans 6:23

5:14 *Nevertheless death reigned from Adam until Moses, even over those who had not sinned in the likeness of Adam's offense, who is a type of Him who was to come.*
5:15 *But the free gift is not like the transgression. For if by the transgression of the one the many died, much more did the grace of God and the gift by the grace of the one Man, Jesus Christ, abound to the many.*
5:16 *And the gift is not like that which came through the one who sinned; for on the one hand the judgment arose from one transgression resulting in condemnation, but on the other hand the free gift arose from many transgressions resulting in justification.*
5:17 *For if by the transgression of the one, death reigned through the one, much more those who receive the abundance of grace and of the gift of righteousness will reign in life through the One, Jesus Christ.*
5:18 *So then as through one transgression there resulted condemnation to all men, even so through one act of righteousness there resulted justification of life to all men.*
5:19 *For as through the one man's disobedience the many were made sinners, even so through the obedience of the One the many will be made righteous.*
5:20 *And the Law came in that the transgression might increase; but where sin increased, grace abounded all the more,*
5:21 *that, as sin reigned in death, even so grace might reign through righteousness to eternal life through Jesus Christ our Lord."*

There are two men — Adam and Christ. There are two acts; one, a self-willed rebellion, disobedience — Adam's sin. The other was a self-sacrificial act of obedience. There are two results: death and life. And there are two reigns (or kingdoms): death reigning and believers reigning in life. Perhaps the keyword in these verses is "one." Paul uses the word twelve times. One sin; Adam's sin brought condemnation. One act of righteousness; the cross of Jesus Christ brings life. Paul is laying out a simple but profound argument. We were condemned in Adam. We are justified in the last Adam — Jesus Christ. Just as Adam's sin was charged to our account, so Christ's act of righteousness was charged to our account.

Paul speaks of imputation, which helps us understand this matter of justification. "Imputation" means that these things are charged to our account. There are three imputations in the Bible. Two of them are here in Romans Chapter 5. The unregenerate man, our flesh, does not like imputation; it rebels against these truths. The first truth is that Adam's sin was charged to the race. That is why I did not have to teach my children how to sin. We are born into sin. The second imputation is of our sin to Christ. When Christ died on the cross, it was not for His sin. "He made Him who knew no sin to be sin on our behalf"[178] on the cross. Isaiah said, "although He had done no violence, nor was any deceit found in His mouth, yet "the Lord was pleased to crush Him."[179] Our sin was placed on Christ. The third imputation is that His righteousness is charged to our account. Paul develops this concept in almost

---

178   2 Corinthians 5:21
179   Isaiah 53:9-10

every verse in this section. Paul says it more succinctly in 1 Corinthians: "For since by a man came death, by a man also came the resurrection of the dead. For as in Adam all die, so also in Christ all shall be made alive."[180]

Just as Paul spoke of "much more" in God's love for us, so he uses that same concept in his argument regarding Adam and Christ. Paul compares and then contrasts. "The free gift is not like the transgression. For if by the transgression of the one the many died, <u>much more</u> did the grace of God and the gift by the grace of the one Man, Jesus Christ, abound to the many."[181] He says it again in verse 17. "If by the transgression of the one, death reigned through the one, <u>much more</u> those who receive the abundance of grace and of the gift of righteousness will reign in life through the One, Jesus Christ." Paul's argument can be put simply this way: If Adam's sin was enough to condemn the race, and it was, "much more" Christ's death on the cross is sufficient to bring life.

Paul emphasizes Jesus' humanity. Adam, a man, brought us sin. And there is another man — <u>The</u> Man — who brings eternal life. Jesus' humanity is emphasized even as He is the leader of the new race. How did I get into Adam? I was born into Adam. How do I get into Christ? I am born again by the resurrection of Jesus Christ. Peter opened his epistle, "Blessed be the God and Father of our Lord Jesus Christ, who according to His great mercy has caused us to be born again to a living

---

180   1 Corinthians 15:21-22
181   Romans 5:15

hope through the resurrection of Jesus Christ."[182] If death was certain in Adam, death reigns. If death was certain in Adam, "much more" life is certain in Christ.

Paul answers an implied question in verses 20 and 21: if Adam and Christ are the whole story, then why the Law? "The Law came in that the transgression might increase; but where sin increased, grace abounded all the more, that, as sin reigned in death, even so grace might reign through righteousness to eternal life through Jesus Christ our Lord."[183] Why the Law? The Law came in that transgression might increase. God's holy Law shows all of us, Jews and Gentiles, we are exactly what Adam was — sinners. Just as we were formerly identified with Adam, we are now identified with a new head — Jesus Christ.

I will conclude with this final thought, if you perish, it will not be because of Adam's sin, it will be because you spurned the gift of salvation in the last Adam — Jesus Christ. Not only in Romans, but all through the Bible, you see this gift offered. "But as many as received Him, to them He gave the right to become children of God"[184] and be born into a new family — God's family.

---

182   1 Peter 1:3
183   Romans 5:20-21
184   John 1:12

Study questions

- What are some of the ways we experience "peace with God" mentioned by Paul in verses 5:1-2?

- Think of an example in your life where your faith was strengthened through trial or tribulation.

- What is the ultimate expression of God's "much more" love for us?

- How does God's love for us while helpless, ungodly, sinners, and enemies of His, give us assurance of the permanence of our faith?

- What is the parallel between Adam and Christ described by Paul in verses 5:12-21?

9
DOES GRACE PROMOTE SIN?

Romans Chapter 6

Justification, God declaring us right, was illustrated in Romans Chapter 4 through Abraham and David. In Romans Chapter 5, Paul says this justification is absolutely secure. Having been justified by faith, we have peace with God. Should trouble come into our lives, and Jesus promised it will, our faith will not be destroyed; it will be refined. If God loved us when we were helpless and ungodly, sinners and enemies of His, much more, we can bask in His love now that we have been declared right with Him. The demonstration of the love of God is the cross. And Paul gave us the analogy between Adam and Christ. Adam's one act of disobedience brought ruin; Jesus Christ's one act of obedience at the Cross brings life.

Our response to these truths should be to praise the Lord, to rejoice. But man is so sinful and depraved that he asks in Chapter 6, verse 1, "Are we to continue in sin that grace might increase?" Paul responds, "May it never be (*me genoito*)!" Absolutely not! In verse 15, he raises the question again, "What then? Shall we sin because we are not under law but under grace?" *Me genoito!* In both cases, Paul rejects it as wrong-hearted, and then he refutes it as wrong-headed. His response to these two parallel questions forms the two great sections of Romans Chapter 6: verses 1-14 — Union with Christ; and verses 15-23 — Slavery to God.

Union with Christ – 6:1-14

> **6:1** *"What shall we say then? Are we to continue in sin that grace might increase?*
> **6:2** *May it never be! How shall we who died to sin still live in it?"*

Paul responds, "How could you say such a thing?" That is the heart of Paul in responding to this question. He brings it up because he has heard it many times: "Well, if it is true that we are saved by grace, then we can just sin!" Paul says, *me genoito!* I purposely use the Greek phrase *"me genoito"* because it is important to see and feel the question and answer. There is a dialogue that is going on throughout Romans. Paul uses this phrase ten times, and you can follow a big part of his logic by tracing its use.

If you preach the gospel of Jesus Christ, this question will be raised: "Well, if we are not saved by works or the Law, we can just go and sin!" Sometimes it is even raised to the height of saying, "Not only can we sin, but we should sin 'that grace might increase.'"[185] Paul raised this same question earlier

---

185 Romans 6:1

in Romans Chapter 3, "Why not say (as we are slanderously reported, and as some affirm that we say), 'Let us do evil that good may come?'"[186] Recall that Paul did not even waste a *me genoito* there, he just said, "their condemnation is just."[187] Paul was used to this question. Wherever the cross of Christ is proclaimed, this wrong-hearted, wrong-headed question will come up. It is even asked by people who call themselves Christians, "Well, then I could just live how I like." Our response should be, "God's Son died for you. *Me genoito.* Do not even think of saying it."

It is not that Christians never sin. Yes, Christians sin, but we say that with heartbreak. "If we say that we have no sin, we are deceiving ourselves... [But,] if we confess our sins, He is faithful and righteous to forgive us our sins" because "the blood of Jesus His Son cleanses us from all sin."[188] The gospel of grace promotes a hatred of sin. "Abhor what is evil; cling to what is good."[189] "Hate evil, you who love the Lord."[190]

"Walk in newness of life"

6:3 *"Or do you not know that all of us who have been baptized into Christ Jesus have been baptized into His death?*
6:4 *Therefore we have been buried with Him through baptism into death, in order that as Christ was raised from*

---

186 Romans 3:8
187 *Id.*
188 1 John 1:7-9
189 Romans 12:9
190 Psalms 97:10

the dead through the glory of the Father, so we too might walk in newness of life.

6:5 For if we have become united with Him in the likeness of His death, certainly we shall be also in the likeness of His resurrection,"

You and I are united to Christ. He has died, never to die again, once for all.[191] At conversion, when you come to Christ, you are identified with Him. Not only did Christ die for us, we died with Him. This is what we mean when we say, "the identification of the Christian with Christ." That is the basis for justification. That is also the basis for "sanctification." Starting at Romans Chapter 6, we enter a new section of Romans: God's method of sanctifying His blood-bought children.

The gospel is the power of God for salvation! Salvation in the Bible means deliverance. The Bible speaks of salvation both past, present and future. Up to now, we have been emphasizing the past; Christ died for us! In so doing, He declared us righteous, which is justification. Having been justified, we have peace and deliverance from the penalty of sin. Presently, we are being delivered from the power of sin, being set apart for Him. This is sanctification. In the future, we will be delivered from the very presence of sin. We will be like Him; new bodies, perfect. This is glorification. Justification is in the past, sanctification in the present, and glorification in the future. Stated another way, we were delivered from the penalty of sin in the past; we are being delivered from the power of sin now; and in the future, we will be delivered from the very presence of sin.

191   *See* Romans 6:9-10

When you see the word salvation in the Bible, it is not always referring to the past — justification. Sometimes it is referring to the future — glorification. For instance, in Romans Chapter 13, Paul says, "for now salvation is nearer to us than when we believed."[192] Salvation is now nearer to us than it was yesterday. We are one day closer to that day when Jesus Christ will take us home, and we will be changed in a moment. In the twinkling of an eye, we will be delivered from the presence of sin. In between those two points, the past and the future, God is in the process of sanctifying us. Jesus prayed, "Sanctify them in the truth; Your word is truth."[193]

What was the basis for justification? The cross. What is the basis for sanctification? The cross. When Christ died, we died. When Christ was buried, we were buried. When Christ arose, we arose. We were co-crucified, co-buried, and co-raised. Paul states it clearly over and over in these few verses. You can see it stated in Paul's other epistles as well. In Galatians, he writes, "I have been crucified with Christ; and it is no longer I who live, but Christ lives in me; and the life which I now live in the flesh I live by faith in the Son of God, who loved me and delivered Himself up for me."[194]

---

192 Romans 13:11
193 John 17:17
194 Galatians 2:20

No longer slaves to sin

> **6:6** *"knowing this, that our old self was crucified with Him, that our body of sin might be done away with, that we should no longer be slaves to sin;*
>
> **6:7** *for he who has died is freed from sin.*
>
> **6:8** *Now if we have died with Christ, we believe that we shall also live with Him,*
>
> **6:9** *knowing that Christ, having been raised from the dead, is never to die again; death no longer is master over Him.*
>
> **6:10** *For the death that He died, He died to sin, once and for all; but the life that He lives, He lives to God.*
>
> **6:11** *Even so consider yourselves to be dead to sin, but alive to God in Christ Jesus."*

Verse 6 of Romans gives us the result of our identification with Christ. "Knowing this that our old self was crucified with Him, in order that our body of sin might be done away with, so that we should no longer be slaves to sin."[195] Paul states it negatively – no longer a slave to sin. He states it positively in verse 4, "so we too might walk in newness of life."[196] "If anyone is in Christ, he is a new creature; the old things have passed away; behold, new things have come." [197]

Paul reiterates this emphasis on "life" in verses 9 and 10, "knowing that Christ, having been raised from the dead, is never to die again; death no longer is master over Him. For the death that He died, He died to sin once for all; but the life that He lives,

---

195 Romans 6:6
196 Romans 6:4
197 2 Corinthians 5:17

He lives to God."[198] Our Savior is alive! Never to die again. We are in Christ. Yes, our bodies will wear out, but we have eternal life. We live in Christ; on the resurrection side of the cross. He is life. John begins his gospel, "In Him was life."[199] Jesus said, "I came that they might have life, and have it abundantly."[200] "This is eternal life," Jesus prayed, "that they might know You … and Jesus Christ whom you have sent."[201]

Now, verse 11: "Even so, consider yourselves to be dead to sin but alive to God in Christ Jesus." Paul is not telling us to do anything. He is simply saying to consider it done. Consider it true! God said it, believe it. It is an exhortation to faith. When Christ died, you died. When Christ arose, you arose. Consider it so and "walk in newness of life"[202] as a new creature, as a child of God.

Present yourself to God – 6:12-14

6:12 *"Therefore do not let sin reign in your mortal body that you obey its lusts,*

6:13 *and do not go on presenting the members of your body to sin as instruments of unrighteousness; but present yourselves to God as those alive from the dead, and your members as instruments of righteousness to God.*

6:14 *For sin shall not be master over you, for you are not under law, but under grace."*

---

198 Romans 6:9-10
199 John 1:4
200 John 10:10
201 John 17:3
202 Romans 6:4

These three verses are a kind of a central exhortation; central in that they are between the two principal sections of Chapter 6. Paul basically says, "No, do not sin. Present yourself to Him." "Do not go on presenting the members of your body to sin as instruments of unrighteousness; but present yourselves to God."[203] Present your members to God; your hands, your feet, your eyes, your ears, your sexuality, everything. This verse is a foreshadowing of the first real imperative in Romans, which we will not get to until Romans Chapter 12. Paul explains the gospel all the way through Chapter 11, and only then in Chapter 12 he says, "I urge you therefore, brethren, ... to present your bodies a living and holy and sacrifice."[204]

Christian truth is the basis for Christian living. If you want to see people grow, do not just harangue them with what they ought to do; proclaim what Christ did! Always in Paul's letters, first he gives truth, and then the implications of the truth. He presents doctrine first, then duty. There are eleven chapters of truth in Romans before Paul starts with an exhortation of how we should respond. This is a good pattern for us.

In verse 14, Paul writes, "Sin shall not be master over you, for you are not under law, but under grace." Often, we think if we are not under the law, people will have the freedom to sin. Paul calls for absolute obedience to God on the basis of grace. You are not under law but under grace. This sets the table for the second half of Romans Chapter 6, where Paul argues for slavery to God.

---

203 Romans 6:13
204 Romans 12:1

Slavery to God – 6:15-23

> **6:15** *"What then? Shall we sin because we are not under law but under grace? May it never be!*
>
> **6:16** *Do you not know that when you present yourselves to someone as slaves for obedience, you are slaves of the one whom you obey, either of sin resulting in death, or of obedience resulting in righteousness?*
>
> **6:17** *But thanks be to God that though you were slaves of sin, you became obedient from the heart to that form of teaching to which you were committed,*
>
> **6:18** *and having been freed from sin, you became slaves of righteousness."*

Paul begins by asking again, "What then? Shall we sin because we are not under law but under grace? May it never be (*me genoito*)."[205] Paul rejected this question earlier as wrong-hearted;[206] he refutes it now through the rest of Chapter 6 as wrongheaded. "Do you not know that when you present yourselves to someone as slaves for obedience, you are slaves of the one whom you obey, either of sin resulting in death, or of obedience resulting in righteousness?"[207] Paul is calling for slavery to God; an absolute obedience. When you call people to slavery, there will be those who say, "that is legalism" or "that is demeaning." Maybe that is going on in your heart right now. Paul spends the rest of this chapter saying, "Yes, I am calling for slavery," but "No, it is not demeaning — it is freedom."

---

205 Romans 6:15
206 Romans 6:1-11
207 Romans 6:16

Paul's theme in this whole section is that you are a slave to whom you obey. It is not a question of whether or not we are a slave — we are either a slave to sin or a slave to God. Slavery to sin leads to bondage, misery, and death. Slavery to God leads not to bondage, but freedom; not misery, but joy. It sets us free from death to life. Satan hates this truth. He is the father of lies. Satan tells us, "You can be free in sin; free to sin; free from God." Man is so gullible, so deceivable, that we believe Satan even though all the evidence around us is so clear that sin's so-called freedom leads to bondage, addiction, and misery. Jesus Christ said, "everyone who commits sin is the slave of sin."[208] But "If ... the Son will set you free, you will be free indeed."[209] Satan is the one who enslaves; Christ is the one who sets us free.

And so, Paul bursts into praise:

> "Thanks be to God that though you were slaves of sin, you became obedient from the heart to that form of teaching to which you were committed, and having been freed from sin, you became slaves of righteousness."[210]

I love the phrase, "though you were slaves of sin, you became obedient from the heart."[211] When Jesus Christ transforms our life, when we come to Christ, we are changed from the inside out. We are new creatures. Sanctification is not a bunch of external rules we must follow. It is an internal dynamic

---

208 John 8:34
209 John 8:36. John 8:31-38 is a parallel passage to this section of Romans.
210 Romans 6:17-18
211 Romans 6:17

of walking in newness of life, "yoked up" with Jesus Christ. "Come to Me, all who are weary and heavy-laden, and I will give you rest. Take my yoke upon you ... and you will find rest for your souls."[212] Obedience from the heart is the dynamic of the Christian life.

Romans 6:19-23

6:19 *"I am speaking in human terms because of the weakness of your flesh. For just as you presented your members as slaves to impurity and to lawlessness, resulting in further lawlessness, so now present your members as slaves to righteousness, resulting in sanctification.*

6:20 *For when you were slaves of sin, you were free in regard to righteousness.*

6:21 *Therefore what benefit were you then deriving from the things of which you are now ashamed? For the outcome of those things is death.*

6:22 *But now having been freed from sin and enslaved to God, you derive your benefit, resulting in sanctification, and the outcome, eternal life.*

6:23 *For the wages of sin is death, but the free gift of God is eternal life in Christ Jesus our Lord."*

Paul continues to reiterate here that there are two slaveries. The first one, slavery to sin, results in death. Using the term "benefit," which is translated from the Greek word for fruit. Paul asks, what benefit ("fruit") were you receiving "from the things of which you are now ashamed?" What was the result

---
212 Mathew 11:28-29

of slavery to sin? "The outcome of those things is death."[213] In contrast, the benefit (fruit) you derive from slavery to God results in sanctification and eternal life.[214]

I encourage you to take your place as a slave of Jesus Christ. The very first verse of Romans begins, "Paul, a bond-servant [slave -*duolos*] of Christ Jesus."[215] He is not at all ashamed to be called a slave of Christ. There is joy in slavery to Christ. There is freedom in saying, "I am yours." We have been bought with a price. We are not our own. There is great freedom in that. We are not just following the words of the Apostle Paul here. Jesus said, "I have come … not to do My will, but the will of Him who sent me."[216] The things that I speak, "I do not speak on My own initiative," but "I speak just as the Father has told me.[217] As the perfect man, Jesus is the perfect example for us not to go our own way and do our own thing, but to live for Him, speak for Him, teach what He taught. "My food," Jesus said, "is to do the will of Him who sent me."[218] This is the dynamic of healthy Christian living because you and I are united with Christ.

I close with this thought lest we begin to think that obedience is the way to eternal life. In verse 23, Paul proclaims so clearly, "For the wages of sin is death, but the free gift of God is eternal

---

213 Romans 6:21
214 *See* Romans 6:22
215 Romans 1:1
216 John 6:38
217 John 12:49-50; *see also* John 5:19 and 8:28
218 John 4:34

life in Christ Jesus our Lord."[219] Sanctification is an integral part of the gospel, but we do not earn salvation; it is a "free gift" — unmerited.

---

219 Romans 6:23

Study questions

- If we are saved by grace, why aren't we free to sin and just live our lives how we like?

- What does it mean to "walk in the newness of life" (6:4)?

- How does sanctification, being presently delivered from the power of sin, differ from justification?

- Paul calls on us to be "enslaved to God" (6:22). How does that, in fact, set you free, and what are the implications for living a Christ-like life?

10

THE CHRISTIAN AND THE LAW

Romans Chapter 7

In Chapter 1:17 through Chapter 3:20, Paul indicted man's unrighteousness. It can be summed up by his statement in Chapter 6, "The wages of sin is death."[220] In the next section, Chapter 3:21 to 5:21, Paul establishes the foundation of our faith, "But the free gift of God is eternal life in Christ Jesus our Lord."[221] Christ delivered us from the penalty of sin – "justification." Now in Romans Chapters 6 through 8, Paul explains how Christ delivers us from the power of sin – "sanctification."

We have seen that not only did Christ die for us, we died with Christ. This great deliverance from the power of sin is tied to our identification with Christ. Another way to think of this is that when Christ died, I died, and I am delivered from Adam's race — Romans Chapter 5. When Christ died, I died, and He delivered me from sin as a master – Romans Chapter 6. And

---

220 Romans 6:23
221 *Id.*

when Christ died, I died, and He, therefore, delivered me from the Law, which is what we will now see in Romans Chapter 7.

Introduction to Chapter 7

Romans Chapter 7 teaches us that we are delivered, set free, from the Law. Paul writes in Galatians, "Christ redeemed us from the curse of the Law, having become a curse for us – for it is written, 'cursed is anyone who hangs on a tree.'"[222] One of the advantages of knowing Romans is that as you read Paul's other letters, you can refer back to Romans to understand better the basis behind many of his statements. This verse in Galatians is a great statement, and it stands alone. But we will better understand the basis for it as we read Chapter 7 of Romans.

Chapter 7 mentions the Law or commandment nearly thirty times. You will find the word Law or commandment in every verse from verses 1 through 14. We will learn what the Law can do and what the Law cannot do. Romans Chapter 6 asks, does grace promote sin? Paul says, "May it never be (*Me genoito*)!" Chapter 7 asks, can the Law prevent sin? Again, he answers, *Me genoito* — No!

Paul has made three statements about the Law up to now in Romans that are very shocking to Jewish ears and very shocking to religious ears. We can use those statements to outline Chapter 7.

---

222 Galatians 3:13

- Chapter 3, "By the works of the Law no flesh will be justified in His sight."[223]
- Chapter 5, not only will the Law not justify anyone, "the Law came in that the transgression might increase!" [224]
- Chapter 6, "You are not under Law, but under grace."[225] The Law could not justify anybody. The Law causes sin to increase, and we are not under the Law. These are all shocking statements!

Romans Chapter 7 illuminates these three statements and expands and explains them. We are going to look at them in reverse order. The first section of Romans 7, verses 1 through 6, explains why we are not under the Law — Paul's statement in Romans 6. The second section of Chapter 7, verses 7 through 13, responds to Paul's statement in Romans 5 — what the law *can* do. And then, the balance of Chapter 7, verses 14 through 25, tells us what the law *cannot* do.

We have been released from the Law — 7:1-6

7:1 *"Or do you know, brethren (for I am speaking to those who know the law), that the law has jurisdiction over a person as long as he lives?*

7:2 *For the married woman is bound by law to her husband while he is living; but if her husband dies, she is released from the law concerning the husband.*

---

223 Romans 3:20
224 Romans 5:20
225 Romans 6:14

7:3 *So then if, while her husband is living, she is joined to another man, she shall be called an adulteress; but if her husband dies, she is free from the law, so that she is not an adulteress, though she is joined to another man.* **7:4** *Therefore, my brethren, you also were made to die to the Law through the body of Christ, that you might be joined to another, to Him who was raised from the dead, that we might bear fruit for God."*

We have been released from the Law. Paul says it three times in this short section, verses 2, 3, and 6. He begins by saying, "Do you not know."[226] Knowledge is key to Christian living. When Paul asked, "Do you not know," often he is concerned that we, in fact, do not know. He asked this question in Romans Chapter 6.[227] He asks it again here, "Do you not know, brethren … that the Law has jurisdiction over a person as long as he lives?"[228] But death ends the relationship. When Christ died, we died, and we died to the Law. Paul has previously explained that when Christ died, we were delivered from Adam's race. We are delivered from our old master – sin. Now he says, when Christ died, we died, and we are delivered from the Law. One of the things that can make it difficult to understand this part of Romans is that sometimes Paul is speaking of the Law (the body of decrees found in the first five books of the Old Testament – the "Torah"), and other times he just speaks of "law" like a moral principle.

---

226 Romans 7:1
227 *See* Romans 6:3 and 16
228 Romans 7:1

In verses 2 and 3, Paul gives us a simple analogy that we can all understand; that of a married woman. This is an analogy, and an analogy is never perfect, but it is instructive. When a man and a woman unite in marriage, the two become one. They are husband and wife. God said it at the beginning: For this reason, leave, cleave — the two become one flesh.[229] If her husband dies, the wife dies. She does not literally die, but she is no longer a wife and is free to wed another man. In the same way, Paul explains that when Christ died, we died. We are now free to be wed, not to the Law, but to another — the resurrected Christ who will never die again. "Therefore, my brethren, you also were made to die to the Law through the body of Christ, that you might be joined to another, to Him who was raised from the dead, that we may bear fruit for God."[230]

We are set free from the Law "that we might bear fruit for God;"[231] for holy living. God's purpose in every Christian's life is that we bear fruit. Jesus said, "You did not choose Me, but I chose you… that you should go and bear fruit, and that your fruit should remain."[232] If He has called you to Himself, He has called you to bear fruit. God is glorified when we bear fruit. God wants us wed to the risen Christ to bear much fruit for His glory, "the fruit of the Spirit is love, joy, peace, patience, kindness, goodness, faithfulness, gentleness, self-control."[233] This is Christ-like living; the life of Christ manifested. Where there is life, there will be fruit. Christ is the one who bears the

---

229 See Genesis 2:24
230 Romans 7:4
231 Id.
232 John 15:16
233 Galatians 5:22-23

fruit. He is the vine,[234] but we are connected to Him, and we bear much fruit to His glory.

I was talking to a young businessman, and he was eager to grow as a Christian. He had recently come to Christ, and while we had breakfast together, I challenged him to read Romans repeatedly. He said, "Ok," and he read and re-read it. Jesus said, "If you abide in Me, and My Words abide in you ... you [will] bear much fruit."[235] As a young Christian, he began to grow and he gave himself to the study of Romans. He told me how he was on a business trip with another businessman and how this man went to church but did not really know Christ. They were talking about life, and my young friend quoted the fruit of the Spirit to him — "the fruit of the spirit is love, joy, peace, patience, kindness, goodness, faithfulness, gentleness, self-control."[236] The other businessman said, "That's what I want. That is what I want for my children." He asked my friend, "How did you know that?" It is because my friend spends time in God's word. He abides in it, and he had an opportunity to share it because his life is showing that he is in God's word.

7:5 *"For while we were in the flesh, the sinful passions, which were aroused by the Law, were at work in the members of our body to bear fruit for death.*
7:6 *But now we have been released from the Law, having died to that by which we were bound, so that we serve in newness of the Spirit and not in oldness of the letter."*

234 *See* John 15:1
235 John 15:7-8
236 Galatians 5:22-23

In verses 5 and 6, Paul glances back at our life in the flesh before we were born again. "But now we have been released from the Law."[237] We are wed (joined) to the risen Christ "to serve in newness of the Spirit."[238] We have the freedom of bearing fruit for God. We will see more of this in Romans Chapter 8, but here in the first six verses of Chapter 7 is the doctrinal foundation for our deliverance from the Law.

What the law can do — 7:7-13

Paul said in Chapter 5, "The Law came in that the transgression [sin] might increase."[239] In this next section of Chapter 7, verses 7 through 13, Paul explains what he means by that. Paul has said a lot of negative things about the Law. In Romans Chapter 4, he said, "the Law brings about wrath."[240] In 1 Corinthians, Paul said, "the power of sin is the law."[241] In 2 Corinthians, he calls the Law "the ministry of death."[242] Two verses later, he calls it "the ministry of condemnation."[243] Given all those negative statements, Paul raises the question here in Chapter 7:7, is the Law sinful? He raises it again in verse 13, "Therefore did that which is good become a cause of death for me?" He answers both times, *"Me genoito"* "May it never be!"[244] These two verses are bookends to this section.

---

237 Romans 7:6

238 *Id.*

239 Romans 5:20

240 Romans 4:15

241 1 Corinthians 15:56

242 2 Corinthians 3:7

243 2 Corinthians 3:9

244 To put what Paul says about the Law in context, it is good to remember that the Psalmist said, *"Oh how I love your Law, it is my mediation day and night."* Psalms 119:97.

7:7 *"What shall we say then? Is the Law sin? May it never be! On the contrary, I would not have come to know sin except through the Law; for I would not have known about coveting if the Law had not said, 'You shall not covet.'* **7:8** *But Sin, taking opportunity through the commandment, produced in me coveting of every kind; for apart from the Law sin is dead."*

Paul said earlier, "through the Law comes the knowledge of sin."[245] It is as if we might not realize some things are sin if God's word did not say, "Yes, it is!" It was not that it was not sinful, but we would have been blind to it. The Law shows sin to be sin. Paul picks the tenth commandment as an example — "you shall not covet."[246] This is one we might neglect. I have wondered if when Saul met Jesus Christ on the road to Damascus, he was already under conviction, as is usual in our lives when we are being drawn towards Christ. As a good Pharisee, he was trying to keep all the laws, but even the tenth commandment was gnawing away at him. "You shall not covet your neighbor's house, ... your neighbor's wife, ... or his donkey."[247]

People tell me sometimes, "Oh, I keep the Law, I keep the commandments." I say to them, "Do you? Do you perfectly love the Lord your God?" We could start with the first commandment and go right down the list. Can you say, "I have never committed adultery?" Jesus said, "I say to you, that everyone

---

245 Romans 3:20
246 Exodus 20:17
247 *Id.*

who looks on a woman to lust for her"[248] is as guilty as if you have committed adultery.

The Law not only informs us of sin, but indwelling sin uses the Law to produce sin. It is as if a prohibition arouses the sin in us to do sin. A sign says, "Wet paint. Do not touch!" and we are tempted to touch. The problem is not with the sign. The problem is within us. "Sinful passions … were aroused by the Law."[249] A New Testament scholar, F.F. Bruce, tells a story of an old deacon who did not like the Ten Commandments posted on the wall of the church. The old man said, "They put so many ideas into people's heads."[250]

> **7:9** *"And I was once alive apart from the Law; but when the commandment came, sin became alive, and I died;*
> **7:10** *and this commandment, which was to result in life, proved to result in death for me;*
> **7:11** *for sin, taking opportunity through the commandment, deceived me, and through it killed me.*
> **7:12** *So then, the Law is holy, and the commandment is holy and righteous and good.*
> **7:13** *Therefore did that which is good become a cause of death for me? May it never be! Rather it was sin, in order that it might be shown to be sin by effecting my death through that which is good, that through the commandment sin might become utterly sinful."*

---

248 Mathew 5:28
249 Romans 7:5
250 Bruce, F.F. (1985). *Romans*. InterVarsity Press, p. 132

Bible scholars debate what Paul means here, but I think he was saying that I was once alive before the commandment, and then the commandment came, and I died. I think Paul is not speaking theologically but practically. In Paul's smug, arrogant pre-Christ days, he was alive, he thought. He was "a Pharisee, a son of Pharisees;"[251] "as to the ... Law, found blameless."[252] But when the commandments really hit home, and he realized his sinfulness, he died. He saw his need for Christ. Paul wrote in Galatians that the very function of the Law is to be "our tutor to lead us to Christ."[253] Is sin the Law's fault? *Me genoito!* "The Law ... is holy and righteous and good,"[254] because it shows sin to be "utterly sinful."[255] It can break us of our pride and self-righteousness and drive us to the grace of God found in the Savior.

What the Law cannot do — 7:14-25

This final section of Chapter 7 is as if Paul is responding to the questioner asking, "Well, if the Law cannot justify, can it sanctify?" Paul answers clearly, "No." These verses are autobiographical. Paul is telling of his own experience. In this section, he uses "I," "me," "my," and "myself" thirty-eight times. It is intensely personal and tells of Paul's lonely, defeated failing struggle. I believe every Christian can relate to his struggle.

---

251 Acts 23:6
252 Philippians 3:6
253 Galatians 3:24
254 Romans 7:12
255 Romans 7:13

7:14 *"For we know that the Law is spiritual; but I am of flesh, sold into bondage to sin.*

7:15 *For that which I am doing, I do not understand; for I am not practicing what I would like to do, but I am doing the very thing I hate.*

7:16 *But if I do the very thing I do not wish to do, I agree with the Law, confessing that it is good.*

7:17 *So now, no longer am I the one doing it, but sin which indwells me."*

I worked on a crew of men for four years, and most of them were non-Christians. I was learning how to boldly speak of my faith to them. When you work day in and day out with people, you get many opportunities. There was one man on the crew of maybe 15 of us who, because of his lifestyle and everything about him, I would have thought least likely to respond. But I had the privilege of seeing him come to know Jesus Christ. I gave him a Bible, and we would meet away from work and study the Bible together. I told him to read Romans. He came to me about two weeks later. He had stopped in Romans Chapter 7 and said, "I can really relate to this guy Paul."

Whether we are weak or strong, young or mature in the Lord, there is a sense in which we can all relate to Paul's intensely personal struggle. But this should not be our habitual experience. I do not believe Paul's habitual lifestyle was of a lonely struggle and focus on himself. Romans Chapter 8 is coming. This might have been Paul's experience before he really grasped the first six verses of Chapter 7. Humanly speaking, this is why he wrote the first six verses, that we might know that we have been set free from that lonely, legal struggle and we are wed to the risen Christ. This will be our struggle if we forget that we have died with Christ and are on resurrected ground, set free from the Law. In other words, if we try to live the Christian life by the Law and by our own strength, this kind of struggle will be habitual. God's holy standards, His moral laws, are to be obeyed, not in the flesh, but in the Holy Spirit.

It should be noted that there is no mention in this section of the Holy Spirit. In writing about Romans 7, Bishop Moule called it "this absolute and eloquent silence" regarding the Holy Spirit.[256] It is always dangerous to make an argument from silence. But we are going to see the ministry of the Holy Spirit in full bloom in Romans Chapter 8 — The Spirit of Christ lives within us.[257] The dynamic of the victorious Christian life is not struggling on our own. "I have been crucified with Christ, and It is no longer I who live, but Christ lives in me.[258]

> **7:18** *"For I know that nothing good dwells in me, that is, in my flesh; for the wishing is present in me, but the doing of the good is not.*
> **7:19** *For the good that I wish, I do not do; but I practice the very evil that I do not wish.*
> **7:20** *But if I am doing the very thing I do not wish, I am no longer the one doing it, but sin which dwells in me."*

256 Moule, Handley C.G. (1906). *The Epistle of St. Paul to the Romans,* page 194.
257 *See, e.g.,* Romans 8: 9-11.
258 Galatians 2:20

Verses 18 through 20 cover the same ground as in verses 14 through 17 above, which is what is happening in Paul's own experience. Verses 17 and 20 both end, "but sin which dwells in me." The problem is indwelling sin, and in both cases, Paul says, "no longer am I the one doing it."[259] "If I am doing the very thing I do not wish, I am no longer the one doing it, but sin which dwells in me."[260]

Paul learned two things that we should learn, "Nothing good dwells in me, that is, in my flesh; for the wishing is present in me, but the doing of the good is not."[261] Put another way, Paul learned that there is no good in what we sometimes call the old nature (in the flesh). He also learned that there is no power in his new nature.

Looking ahead, we will see that the power is in the Holy Spirit who indwells us. That is not to negate that Paul's struggle is very real, and he shares that struggle here under the inspiration of the Spirit for our instruction and encouragement.

> **7:21** *"I find then the principle that evil is present in me, the one who wishes to do good.*
> **7:22** *For I joyfully concur with the law of God in the inner man,*
> **7:23** *but I see a different law in the members of my body, waging war against the law of my mind, and making me a prisoner of the law of sin which is in my members.*

---

259   Romans 7:17
260   Romans 7:20
261   Romans 7:18

> **7:24** *Wretched man that I am! Who will set me free from*
> *the body of this death?*
> **7:25** *Thanks be to God through Jesus Christ our Lord! So*
> *then, on the one hand I myself with my mind am serving the*
> *law of God, but on the other, with my flesh the law of sin.*"

It is as if Paul says, "Yes, I died to sin. Yes, I am a new creature. Yes, my inner man joyfully concurs with God's law. But no, that does not mean the struggle is over." Experience tells us this, Romans teaches this, and the Bible speaks of this throughout. There is still this different law "in the members of my body;"[262] "in my flesh."[263] "Evil is present in me."[264] Finally, Paul cries out, "Wretched man that I am! Who will set me free from the body of this death?"[265] I believe every Christian can relate to Paul's struggle and look ahead to that day when we will be set free from the very presence of sin — glorification.

That does not mean that we should live in habitual defeat. Paul closes the chapter with these two options: "On the one hand I myself with my mind am serving the law of God, but on the other, with my flesh the law of sin."[266] To put this into perspective within the book of Romans, the two options Paul gives here are living in sin at the end of Chapter 7 or living in Christ in Romans Chapter 8. As a preview, Paul writes, "What the Law could not do, weak as it was through the flesh, God did: sending His own Son in the likeness of sinful flesh and

---

262 Romans 7:23
263 Romans 7:18
264 Romans 7:21
265 Romans 7:24
266 Romans 7:25

as an offering for sin, He condemned sin in the flesh."[267] No wonder Paul bursts into praise, "Thanks be to God through Jesus Christ our Lord."[268]

---

267 Romans 8:3
268 Romans 7:25

Study questions

- How does the analogy of the married women, verses 7:1-4, explain how we have been released from the Law?

- Contrast bearing "fruit for God" with bearing "fruit for death" (7:4-5).

- What can you learn from the personal struggles described by Paul in this chapter? Can you relate to those struggles in your own life?

- Summarize what Paul instructs about what the Law can do and what the Law cannot do.

11

THE MINISTRY OF THE SPIRIT OF GOD

Romans 8:1-27

If I had to pick a favorite chapter in the Bible, it might very well be Romans 8. I am glad I do not have to choose. I was blessed to have Christian parents and grandparents on both sides who loved Jesus Christ. I remember asking my dad what his favorite bible chapter was, and he said Romans 8. So, as a young boy, that was my favorite. I had not even read it yet. As I got to know Romans 8, I can see why he said that, and it has become a dear friend. My grandfather on my dad's side died when I was just a baby. I did not get to know him, but my dad told me that when he died, at the grave, they read Romans 8. I still remember the phone call when my other grandpa died, and my mom and dad sat down and read Romans 8 to each other. My wife and I memorized the chapter together when we were young.

Of course, Romans 8 is not just precious to me personally. Christians all over the world love this chapter. When I was first studying Romans, there was a man teaching Romans on the radio, Donald Grey Barnhouse. He had a very old-fashioned voice, and he was very poetic in the way he would say things. I remember him describing the Bible as a mountain range, the book of Romans as Mount Everest, and Chapter 8 of Romans as the summit. I remember him talking about the gospel as being like a ring; that Romans was the diamond on the ring, and then he said that Romans 8 is the sparkle. Time spent in Romans 8 is time well spent.

Chapter 8 can be divided into two parts. The first section, verses 1 – 27, concern the ministry of the Holy Spirit. The second section, verse 28 to the end, deals with the security of the children of God. There is overlap between the two sections, and they contain much more than just what is mentioned in these descriptions, but that provides a broad outline.

No condemnation – 8:1
Before describing the ministry of the Holy Spirit, Paul begins with the following great truth:

> **8:1** *"There is therefore now no condemnation for those who are in Christ Jesus."*

Romans 8 begins with "no condemnation," and it ends with "no separation." Nothing created "shall be able to separate us from the love of God, which is in Christ Jesus our Lord."[269] No condemnation. No separation. Nobody can separate us from Christ. If that was all the chapter said, that would be

---

269 Romans 8:38-39

enough. We should rejoice in the way the chapter begins and ends with this truth. And in each case, Paul talks about being "in Christ Jesus." Paul uses this phrase, "in Christ Jesus" or "through Christ Jesus" many times in Romans. In Chapter 5, he writes, "We also exult in God through our Lord Jesus Christ."[270] "As sin reigned in death, even so grace might reign through righteousness to eternal life through Jesus Christ our Lord."[271] In Chapter 6 he says, "The wages of sin is death, but the free gift of God is eternal life in Christ Jesus our Lord."[272] And Chapter 7 closes with that great praise, "Thanks be to God through Jesus Christ our Lord."[273] Every blessing of God flows to us in Christ Jesus.

Verse 1 of Chapter 8 is stated much like Paul started Chapter 5, where he said, "Therefore having been justified by faith, we have peace with God."[274] Now he says, "there is now no condemnation for those who are in Christ Jesus."[275] "We have peace"; that is a positive declaration. There is "no condemnation;" that states it negatively. But we do not have to choose between these two verses. Both are the result of this great truth of justification by faith. We have peace with our Creator and absolutely no condemnation. Nobody can bring up past sins. God put our sins "as far as the east is from the west."[276] Oh, there is an accuser of the brethren – Satan, but he is ultimately

---

270 Romans 5:11
271 Romans 5:21
272 Romans 6:23
273 Romans 7:25
274 Romans 5:1
275 Romans 8:1
276 Psalms 103:12

powerless because we have an advocate with the Father, Jesus Christ the Righteous.

Attributes of the ministry of the Holy Spirit

The Holy Spirit was not mentioned in the last half of Romans Chapter 7, but now, in the first twenty-seven verses of Chapter 8, He will be referred to eighteen times. These verses tell us twelve things the Holy Spirit does in our lives, which will be further unfolded for us:

1. The Holy Spirit liberates us from the bondage of sin, 8:2;
2. He empowers us to fulfill the Law's righteous requirement, 8:4;
3. We live according to the Spirit, 8:5-7;
4. The Holy Spirit indwells us, 8:9;
5. He gives life to our spirit, 8:10;
6. He will soon give life to our bodies, 8:11;
7. His indwelling obliges us to live according to His direction, 8:12;
8. The Holy Spirit enables us to put to death the deeds of the body, 8:13;
9. He leads us, 8:14;
10. He gives assurance of our sonship, 8:15 — 16;
11. He, Himself, is the first fruit of our future inheritance, 8:23; and
12. He intercedes for us; He prays for us, 8:26 — 27.

In the following verses, Paul introduces the Holy Spirit.

The Spirit of Life – 8:2

8:2 *"For the law of the Spirit of life in Christ Jesus has set you free from the law of sin and of death."*

The Holy Spirit is the Spirit of Life. He is life-giving. He sets us free. What a contrast from Paul's cry in Romans Chapter 7, "Wretched man that I am! Who will set me free?"[277] Paul now says the Spirit of life has set us free. The very first thing the Holy Spirit does is liberate us; He sets free. The Son of God died and rose again, which is the basis for our salvation. The Spirit of God lives in us; He indwells us and applies salvation subjectively in our experience. Paul has been emphasizing the Son of God through the early chapters because the cross is the basis, the objective foundation, for our deliverance. The Spirit of God is the one who will give us the subjective experience of that deliverance.

Walking in the Spirit – 8:3-4

8:3 *"For what the Law could not do, weak as it was through the flesh, God did: sending His own Son in the likeness of sinful flesh and as an offering for sin, He condemned sin in the flesh,*

8:4 *in order that the requirement of the Law might be fulfilled in us, who do not walk according to the flesh, but according to the Spirit."*

---

277 Romans 7:24

What we could never do, God did. God the Son died for us. God the Spirit lives in us in order that we might live a holy life. Paul puts it this way, "In order that the requirement of the Law might be fulfilled in us, who do not walk according to the flesh, but according to the Spirit."[278] In Chapter 7, Paul says we cannot keep the Law because of indwelling sin. Chapter 8 insists that we can and must follow God's holiness because of the indwelling Spirit. The indwelling Holy Spirit enables us to live a life pleasing to Him.

Paul uses the phrase, "To walk … according to the Spirit."[279] The term walk is one of the most common analogies we find in the New Testament. It is a useful analogy because it is easy for us to understand. It has the idea of a step-by-step, day-by-day lifestyle. We are to "walk by faith, not by sight;"[280] "walk as children of light;"[281] and "walk in love."[282] I remember how my son learned to walk. I wanted him to play baseball, so I was propping him up and gave him a bat to hit the ball. Before he could hit the ball and run down to first base, however, he had to first learn how to walk. When kids learn to walk, they take a step, they stumble and they fall. You pick them back up and they eventually learn to walk. Nobody learns to walk without stumbling. After a while, my son could outrun me. James tells us in Chapter 3, "We all stumble in many ways,"[283]

---

278 Romans 8:4
279 *Id.*
280 2 Corinthians 5:7
281 Ephesians 5:8
282 Ephesians 5:2
283 James 3:2

but we need to get back up and walk in the power of the Holy Spirit day-by-day, step-by-step.

Live according to the Spirit – 8:5-8

8:5 *"For those who are according to the flesh set their minds on the things of the flesh, but those who are according to the Spirit, the things of the Spirit.*

8:6 *For the mind set on the flesh is death, but the mind set on the Spirit is life and peace,*

8:7 *because the mind set on the flesh is hostile toward God; for it does not subject itself to the law of God, for it is not even able to do so;*

8:8 *and those who are in the flesh cannot please God."*

We are to set our mind on the things of the Spirit, not on the things of the flesh. It is a daily moment-by-moment choice, a conscious setting of our mind on the things of the Spirit; the ways of God, the word of God, and the glory of God. To set my mind on the things of the Holy Spirit is to be absorbed with that which pleases Him. Our interests, our purpose, our activities are to be His, grounded in His Word. We follow the promptings of the Holy Spirit step-by-step as we fill our mind with the Holy Word of God, which is "the sword of the Spirit."[284] This is the changed life; walking according to the Spirit. He has made His mind known to us through His Word. We do not merely have to say, "Guide me;" we can open our Bible and ask Him to guide us. As we fill our mind with His Word, we are filled

284 Ephesians 6:17

with His ways, His purposes, His glory. We are filled with "the things of the Spirit."[285]

Those who are in the flesh cannot please God. That is parallel to what Jesus said in John 3, where He used the picture of birth. "Do not marvel that I said to you, 'You must be born again.'"[286] "That which is born of the flesh is flesh; and that which is born of the Spirit is spirit."[287] You must be born again. You must be born of God's Spirit, which occurs when you believe in the Lord Jesus Christ. It is the Spirit who gives life, and without Him, we cannot please God. A person who is in the flesh can go to church, give money, he can try to change his life, but he cannot please God.

The Holy Spirit indwells us – 8:9

> **8:9** "However you are not in the flesh but in the Spirit, if indeed the Spirit of God dwells in you. But if anyone does not have the Spirit of Christ, he does not belong to Him."

The issue is not receiving the Holy Spirit; we are given Him when we believe in Christ. Paul is saying you are not in the flesh, you are in the Spirit because he is writing to Christians. He said, "the Spirit of God dwells in you … If anyone does not have the Spirit of Christ, he does not belong to Him."[288] This is an anchor for your soul. Many Christians think that they

285 Romans 8:5
286 John 3:7
287 John 3:6
288 Romans 8:9

come to Christ, and then they need to later get the Holy Spirit somehow. They say, "I must be born again of the Spirit." But the moment you put your faith in Christ, there is a removal of sin and a bestowal of the Holy Spirit. We know that our sins have been removed and that the Holy Spirit dwells in us because God's Word says so.

I remember once sitting down with a man to tell him about Jesus. It was in a crowded restaurant, and he was very feisty. He was arguing about everything as I tried to explain the gospel to him. I would share some truth and he would come back at me verbally. Every time I said something, he would return with an argument. Finally, I remember in that noisy restaurant, quoting the Bible to him. I told him, "Christ also died for sin once for all, the just for the unjust." [289] I was prepared for him to argue back and there was silence for a long time. In the noisiness of the restaurant, I had the good sense to be quiet.

Finally, he looked at me and said, "Whoa, did you feel that?"

> I said, "What?"
> "A heavy weight just lifted off my shoulders."
> I said, "No, I didn't feel it."
> "Are you sure?" he said, "It was so real."
> I asked him, "Do you believe that Jesus is God's Son?"
> He said, "Yes."
> "Do you believe He died on the cross for you? The Just for the unjust?"
> He said, "Yes."

---

289 1 Peter 3:18

"Do you believe that He rose again for you?"
He said, "Yes." All his arguing was gone.
I told him, "The weight you felt lift off your shoulders
was your sin and your guilt."

The Spirit of God took the Word of God and opened his heart. I have seen many come to Christ, but I had never seen someone experience it in this way. I did not have that same experience when I came to Christ, but I was no less forgiven. This deliverance is not based on how much you feel or experience it but on the clear testimony of God's Word. I rejoiced with my new brother in Christ that he had felt the burden lift. I showed him more verses and I told him, "Whether you feel this way tomorrow or not, your sin is gone!" Your salvation is not based on how you feel; it is based on the unshakeable Word of God. Our feelings come and go. "Heaven and earth will pass away, but My words will not pass away."[290] "Faith comes from hearing, and hearing by the word of Christ."[291]

When you come to Christ, your sin is removed, whether you feel it or not. Somedays, I feel guilty. But I am still forgiven; my sin has been removed. The Holy Spirit dwells in me whether I feel Him or not. I have God's word on it. "You are not in the flesh but in the Spirit, if indeed the Spirit of God dwells in you. But if anyone does not have the Spirit of Christ, he does not belong to Him."[292] The Holy Spirit dwells in every child of God.

---

290 Matthew 24:35
291 Romans 10:17
292 Romans 8:9

The Spirit gives life – 8:10-13

8:10 *"And if Christ is in you, though the body is dead because of sin, yet the spirit is alive because of righteousness.*

8:11 *But if the Spirit of Him who raised Jesus from the dead dwells in you, He who raised Christ Jesus from the dead will also give life to your mortal bodies through His Spirit who indwells you.*

8:12 *So then, brethren, we are under obligation, not to the flesh, to live according to the flesh –*

8:13 *for if you are living according to the flesh, you must die; but if by the Spirit you are putting to death the deeds of the body, you will live."*

My body is just as dead as a non-Christian's in the sense that it is decaying and will die, but the Spirit of life has entered into it, and one day I will get a new body. D. Martyn Lloyd-Jones was a great bible teacher of a different generation in Britain. He was a medical doctor before he began to preach. Commenting on verse 10 as both a physician and a pastor, he wrote, "The moment we enter into this world and begin to live, we also begin to die. Your first breath is one of the last you will ever take. The principle of decay leading to death is in every one of us."[293] We cannot deny that. We may not like to think of the body dying. I still remember my grandson being born. He looked so healthy and vital. But Lloyd-Jones is right; we are all dying physically.

---

293 Lloyd-Jones, D. Martyn (1985). *Romans, Chapters 7:1 — 8:4,* Zondervan Publishing, p. 69

The body is dead because of sin, but the Spirit is alive because of what Christ has done. The Spirit of God, "who raised Jesus from the dead"[294] dwells in us. Jesus Christ will come back for us. "Our citizenship is in heaven, from which also we eagerly wait for a Savior, the Lord Jesus Christ, who will transform the body of our humble state into conformity with the body of His glory, by the exertion of the power that He has even to subject all things to Himself."[295] Someday we are going to get new bodies like His.

The Holy Spirit leads us – 8:14

8:14 *"For all who are being led by the Spirit of God, these are sons of God."*

Because the Holy Spirit opened our eyes, gave us life, raised us up and indwells us, our new obligation is now to live in, and be led by, the Spirit. This is the normal Christian life, to be led by the Holy Spirit. We are not to be self-willed, doing "our own thing," but daily, step-by-step, walking in the Spirit.

Children of God – 8:15-17

8:15 *"For you have not received a spirit of slavery leading to fear again, but you have received a spirit of adoption as sons by which we cry out, 'Abba! Father!'*
8:16 *The Spirit Himself bears witness with our spirit that we are children of God."*

---

294 Romans 8:11
295 Philippians 3:20 – 21

The Spirit bears witness with our spirit that we are children of God, born of the Spirit into God's family. He enables us to say, "Abba, Father."

I remember another man that came to know Jesus Christ. He was a very tough man. He heard the gospel and he responded. He did not have a spiritual background, but I looked at him and asked him, "Why don't you pray and express your gratitude and receive the gift of Christ." He looked at me and said, "I don't know how to pray." I replied, "Prayer is just talking to God," and I felt led by the Spirit to have him pray. I bowed my head and I waited. There was a pause, and then he said, "God, I'm a sinner." I do not remember what he prayed after that, but I have never forgotten those words. He expressed his faith in Christ. We set up an appointment to meet a week later, and I showed him some more Bible verses. The Spirit of God taught him from the Word of God, and the Spirit of truth guided him into the Word of truth. When we were done, I said, "Why don't you pray." He looked at me like, "Who is this guy always asking me to pray?" I bowed my head and he prayed, "Father...." I rejoiced in that because he was born again. The Spirit bore witness with his spirit that he is a child of God.

Suffering of this present time – 8:17-18

Being children of God does not mean that we will not suffer.

> **8:17** *"and if children, heirs also, heirs of God and fellow-heirs with Christ, if indeed we suffer with Him in order that we may also be glorified with Him.*

8:18 *For I consider that the sufferings of this present time are not worthy to be compared with the glory that is to be revealed to us."*

I can address almighty God, "Abba, Father." "If children," we are also "heirs of God and fellow-heirs with Christ."[296] But this does not preclude suffering. "Indeed we suffer with Him in order that we may also be glorified with Him."[297] God never promised us freedom from suffering. It is a false gospel that says if you come to Jesus, everything will be fine in your life. God ties suffering and glory together throughout the Bible. Our Lord Jesus Christ suffered before He entered into His glory. The prophets of old pointed ahead to Him and "predicted the sufferings of Christ and the glories to follow."[298] "The sufferings of this present time are not worthy to be compared with the glory that is to be revealed to us."[299] Suffering is very real, but it does not compare to the glory that awaits us. In 2 Corinthians, Paul states:

"Therefore we do not lose heart, but though our outer man is decaying, yet our inner man is being renewed day by day. For momentary, light affliction is producing for us an eternal weight of glory far beyond all comparison, while we look not at the things which are seen, but at the things which are

296 Romans 8:17
297 *Id.*
298 1 Peter 1:11
299 Romans 8:18

*not seen; for the things which are seen are temporal,
but the things which are not seen are eternal."*[300]

"In the world you have tribulation," Jesus said, "but take
courage; I have overcome the world."[301] The glory that
awaits us will dwarf the very real suffering here on earth.
You may be going through some very real suffering right
now. Take heart from Jesus' words.

The Creation groans – 8:19-22

8:19 *"For the anxious longing of the creation waits eagerly
for the revealing of the sons of God.*
8:20 *For the creation was subjected to futility, not of its
own will, but because of Him who subjected it, in hope*
8:21 *that the creation itself also will be set free from its
slavery to corruption into the freedom of the glory of the
children of God.*
8:22 *For we know that the whole creation groans and
suffers the pains of childbirth together until now."*

The message in Romans 8 applies to the entirety of creation as well as to God's children.   When sin entered the
world, the whole creation was subjected to futility and the
creation groans. The creation suffers from droughts and
other issues; Genesis says both "thorns and thistles" will
grow.[302] The creation is presently not as it should be. It was

---

300 2 Corinthians 4:16-18
301 John 16:33
302 Genesis 3:18

subjected to futility because of Adam's sin. Creation is still groaning. Paul describes it as "the pains of childbirth."[303] When Jesus Christ returns, He will set things right, and He will reveal the sons of God at the second coming.

The first fruits of the Spirit – 8:23-25

8:23 *"And not only this, but also we ourselves, having the first fruits of the Spirit, even we ourselves groan within ourselves, waiting eagerly for our adoption as sons, the redemption of our body.*

8:24 *For in hope we have been saved, but hope that is seen is not hope; for why does one also hope for what he sees?*

8:25 *But if we hope for what we do not see, with perseverance we wait eagerly for it."*

We have "the first fruits of the Spirit."[304] We have the certainty that He is going to finish the work that He started in our life because He left us His Holy Spirit. Ephesians puts it this way: "You were sealed in Him with the Holy Spirit of promise, who is given as a pledge of our inheritance."[305] The word pledge is an economic term; it means "earnest money." We understand earnest money – it is enough money to show that you are earnest – you are serious. Jesus said, I am leaving, but "I will not leave you as orphans."[306] "I will ask the Father, and He will give you another Helper ("*Parakletos*"),"[307] another one like

---

303 Romans 8:22
304 Romans 8:23
305 Ephesians 1:13-14
306 John 14:18
307 John 14:16

Me. God the Son died and ascended to heaven and God the Spirit came at the Day of Pentecost. He is the earnest money, the pledge, the certainty that shows that we can know that God will finish what He started in our lives.

We have the certainty that He will transform our bodies. We groan and suffer now, but we have absolutely certain hope. The sufferings of this present time are like a childbirth labor. They are not pointless. All through the Bible, suffering precedes glory.

The Spirit intercedes for us – 8:26-27

8:26 *"And in the same way the Spirit also helps our weakness; for we do not know how to pray as we should, but the Spirit Himself intercedes for us with groanings too deep for words;*
8:27 *and He who searches the hearts knows what the mind of the Spirit is, because He intercedes for the saints according to the will of God."*

Part of this groaning and suffering is that "we do not even know how to pray as we should, but the Spirit Himself intercedes for us with groanings too deep for words."[308] The Holy Spirit takes our prayers and brings them before the throne of God. He intercedes for His children. God is for us. So, when the accuser comes to you and says, "You don't even pray right," you are able to respond, "It's true, but I have the Spirit of God interceding for me." There is

308 Romans 8:26

no special formula for prayer. You pour your heart out before God, and the Holy Spirit takes it before the throne of God. Every time I pray, I sense my inadequacy, but I have the liberty to just talk to Him and know that the Holy Spirit intercedes for me. No wonder Romans 8 is beloved. It describes the ministry of the Spirit of God on our behalf.

Study questions

- What is the great truth that Paul begins this chapter with?
- List and describe five different attributes of the Holy Spirit mentioned in these verses.
- Give examples of what it looks like to live according to the Spirit (8:5-8).
- Does being a child of God mean that you won't suffer? How can you take heart during momentary suffering?
- What is the "glory that is to be revealed to us" mentioned in verse 8:18?
- What are the "first fruits of the Spirit" (8:23-25).

12

THE SECURITY OF THE CHILDREN OF GOD

Romans 8:28-39

We are secure in Christ. Our security rests not on our own understanding or on our track record; it rests on four great pillars, all of which are found in Romans Chapter 8:

1. The eternal choice of God the Father, 8:28-30.
2. The finished work of God the Son, 8:34.
3. The gracious gift of God the Spirit, 8:23 (discussed in the previous chapter, "The Ministry of the Holy Spirit").
4. The clear statements of God's Word, 8:31-39.

The eternal choice of the Father – 8:28-30

8:28 *"And we know that God causes all things to work together for good to those who love God, to those who are called according to His purpose.*

8:29 *For whom He foreknew, He also predestined to become conformed to the image of His Son, that He might be the first-born among many brethren;*

8.30 *and whom He predestined, these He also called; and whom He called, these He also justified; and whom He justified, these He also glorified."*

"We know that God causes all things to work together for good."[309] Not some things, not most things, but God causes all things to work together for our good. God uses everything for our good "to those who have been called according to His purpose."[310] His purpose includes our good, but more fundamentally Paul says, it is to conform us "to the image of His Son."[311] God is at work in our lives to conform us to the image of His Son.

There are five golden links in verses 29 and 30, which form an unbreakable chain:

- He foreknew.
- He predestined.
- He called.
- He justified.
- He glorified.

The first link is those "whom He foreknew."[312] Paul does not say what He foreknew; he says, whom He foreknew. The phrase the Father "foreknew" us speaks of the personal, intimate knowledge God has of His children. Both the Old and New Testament use the word "knew" in this way. Adam "knew" Eve,

---

309 Romans 8:28
310 *Id.*
311 Romans 8:29
312 Romans 8:29

and they had a child.[313] After the angel appeared to Joseph in a dream in the first chapter of the New Testament, he did not "know" Mary until after Jesus was born.[314] To foreknow speaks of a personal, intimate knowledge.

When the Bible speaks of "foreknowledge," it is not God looking down through history as a bystander to see what is going to happen. God is not waiting to see how your life unfolds or to see how history is going turn out. Those whom He foreknew intimately, these He also predestined. God determined from the start what the outcome would be. In the same way, filled by the Holy Spirit following Pentecost, Peter proclaimed that Jesus was "delivered up by the predetermined plan and foreknowledge of God."[315] God was not caught by surprise. Jesus was not a victim. He came to "give His life a ransom for many"[316] according to God's plan, determined from the beginning. God is in charge.

"And whom He predestined, He also called."[317] This is what theologians call "the effectual call of God." It is not the same as the general or gospel call where we call people to believe in Jesus Christ. When we share the gospel, some listen, many do not. Sometimes our call to the gospel is ineffective. Jesus said, "For many are called, but few are chosen."[318] But the call mentioned in verse 30 is always effective. It is God's call that

---

313 *See* Genesis 4:1
314 *See* Matthew 1:25
315 Acts 2:23
316 Matthew 20:28
317 Romans 8:30
318 Matthew 22:14

opens blinded eyes. You can be a hater of Christ, like Saul of Tarsus, and you hear His voice, and you say, "Who are You, Lord?"[319] Scales fell from his eyes as he was transformed and saved. This is the calling of God. He uses one to implement the other. Romans 10 is going to ask, "How are they going to hear if we do not tell them?"[320] We are called to share the gospel. God uses the gospel call to implement His effectual call. And whom He called, "He justified,"[321] which Paul has been writing about throughout Romans.

The last phrase of verse 30 says, "whom He justified, these He also glorified." This is stated in the past tense. But Paul earlier said we are not yet glorified.[322] As explained previously, justification took place in the past; sanctification is happening in the present, and glorification will take place in the future, where we will be delivered from the very presence of sin. When He appears, we will be like Him.[323] We will have new bodies. This is glorification. But here Paul, guided by the Holy Spirit, uses the past tense – "He also glorified." Only God can do that because with God's purpose, the future is just as certain as the past, and that is what Paul is emphasizing. Nothing can hinder or stop God's eternal purpose.

As a father, I tried not to make promises to my kids as they were growing up unless I knew I could deliver, and I could not always deliver. Things came up and I was not able to fulfill my

---

319   Acts 22:8
320   *See generally* Romans 10:14
321   Romans 8:30
322   *See* Romans 8:17-18
323   *See* 1 John 3:2

promise. But our heavenly Father is God, and nothing "comes up." He will always accomplish what He sets out to do.

From eternity, God has purposed to save His own. Jesus told the twelve disciples, "In My Father's house are many dwelling places; ... I go to prepare a place for you. And if I go and prepare a place for you, I will come again, and receive you to Myself."[324] Jesus meant what He said. He gives these clear statements of His eternal purpose in His children's lives. He will see His sheep safely through. He is not the kind of shepherd that starts off with a hundred and ends up with only ninety-nine.[325] These five great statements in verses 29 and 30 are golden links from eternity to eternity. "Those whom He justified, these He also glorified."[326] It is done!

God is for us – 8:31-33

8:31 *"What then shall we say to these things? If God is for us, who is against us?*

8:32 *He who did not spare His own Son, but delivered Him up for us all, how will He not also with Him freely give us all things?*

8:33 *Who will bring a charge against God's elect? God is the one who justifies."*

Praise God He is for us. To understand verse 31 more clearly, look first at just the phrase at the end, "Who is against us?"

---

324 John 14:2-3
325 *See* Luke 15:4-7
326 Romans 8:30

Satan is against us. He is a slithering serpent;[327] he is a roaring lion;[328] he hates God, and he hates God's children. We are no match for him. Archangel Michael would not even argue with him about the body of Moses.[329] Who is against us? Satan; false cults; the world. If they hated Me, Jesus said, they will hate you.[330] The world is devoted to neutralizing, deceiving, seducing, and destroying Christians. Whole government systems have arisen against us because the god of this world is Satan.

But that reads the verse wrong. It is merely asking who is against us? We need to read it the way it is written — "If God is for us, who is against us?" Nobody of any consequence. God is for us! That changes everything! The eternal, omnipotent Creator is for us! The Sovereign Ruler of the universe is on our side! The "Alpha and the Omega" is for us! If God is for us, then what does it matter who is against us? Who cares who ridicules our faith? What does it matter if our family is against us? Jesus regularly spoke to these kinds of issues. He said, "If anyone wishes to come after Me, he must deny himself, and take up his cross, and follow Me."[331] It may be lonely; we may face opposition, but if God is for us, who is against us?

When I was at the university, I had a desk with a shelf that I could see when I looked up. I put a piece of tape on the edge of the shelf, and I wrote, "If God is for us, who is against us?"[332]

---

327   See Genesis 3:14
328   1 Peter 5:8
329   Jude 1:9
330   See John 15:18, 24-25
331   Matthew 16:24; Luke 9:23
332   Romans 8:31

Joshua and Caleb knew, if the Lord is for us, what does it matter if there are giants in the land?[333] David looked at Goliath and said, "You come to me with a sword, a spear, and a javelin, but I come to you in the name of the Lord."[334]

How do we know that "God is for us?" Because He gave everything for us! "He who did not spare His own Son, but delivered Him up for us all."[335] A blood-stained hill on Calvary attests to it. No matter what is happening in your life right now, God is for us. Who would bring a charge against God's chosen ones? God has chosen us. He has justified us. He has declared us right. Paul wrote earlier in Romans that He loved us when we were His enemies; much more, now that we are His blood-bought children, He continues to love us.[336] Who would dare bring a charge against us?

The finished work of God the Son – 8:34

> **8:34** *"who is the one who condemns? Christ Jesus is He who died, yes, rather who was raised, who is at the right hand of God, who also intercedes for us."*

Verse 34 asks, who can condemn us? The only one who could, Jesus Christ, died for us. He was raised on our behalf. He is seated at the right hand of God. His work is done. He prays for us. He intercedes for us. "He always lives to make intercession"

---

333 *See* 1 Chronicles 20
334 1 Samuel 17:45
335 Romans 8:32
336 *See* Romans 5:10

for us."[337] I try not to say that I am going to pray for someone unless I mean it. If someone asks me to pray, I do not like to lightly say, "Yes, I'll pray." I want to mean it and to follow through. I am ashamed to say that there have been times when I told people I would pray, and I have forgotten to. There is one who never forgets to pray. He always lives to make intercessions for those who draw near to God through Him. It is overwhelming to think that God the Spirit prays for me,[338] and God the Son prays for me.[339] We should never minimize the ministry of intercession. When you and I pray, we are involved in the very activity that our Lord Jesus Christ is involved in, that the Holy Spirit of God is involved in. We do not know how to pray as we should, but the Holy Spirit intercedes for us.[340]

Who will separate us from the love of Christ – 8:35-39

> **8:35** *"Who will separate us from the love of Christ? Will tribulation, or distress, or persecution, or famine, or nakedness, or peril, or sword?*
>
> **8:36** *Just as it is written, 'For Your sake we are being put to death all day long; We were considered as sheep to be slaughtered.'*
>
> **8:37** *But in all these things we overwhelmingly conquer through Him who loved us.*

---

337 Hebrews 7:25
338 *See* Romans 8:27
339 *See* Romans 8:34
340 Romans 8:26

8:38 *For I am convinced that neither death, nor life, nor angels, nor principalities, nor things present, nor things to come, nor powers,*
8:39 *nor height, nor depth, nor any other created thing, shall be able to separate us from the love of God, which is in Christ Jesus our Lord."*

Can anything or anyone separate us from the love of Christ? Paul gives us a thorough list: sickness, war, crime, abuse, financial reversal, famine – nothing can separate us from the love of God. "I am convinced," Paul says, "that neither death, nor life …"[341] Sometimes we are more afraid of what is going to happen in our life than we are about dying and being separated from God's love. Not angels, nor principalities, demons, fallen angels, things that happen presently, nor things to come, nor powers, nor height, nor depth, nor any other created thing, is "able to separate us from the love of God."[342] It is as if Paul writes the list of everything he can think of and then he adds, in case he has forgotten anything, "nor any other created thing."[343] That is the entire universe. There is God the Creator, the triune God, and everything He created. Nothing in the world, nor anything else in the universe, can "separate us from the love of God, which is found in Christ Jesus our Lord."[344]

There is no condemnation. There is no separation. The Father chose us from all eternity. The Son finished the work when He died and rose again. The gracious gift of the Spirit of God

341 Romans 8:38
342 Romans 8:38-39
343 Romans 8:39
344 *Id.*

is the first fruit, the earnest money assuring us that He will finish what He started. And the entire Bible states this in clear statements, of which these verses are among the clearest and most thorough.

Study question

- How do the five "golden links" in verses 8:28-30 form an unbreakable chain demonstrating the security you have in Christ?

- What gives us the assurance that "God is for us" (8:31)? How should that encourage you as you face the challenges of this world?

- Can anything or anyone "separate us from the love of Christ" (8:35)? How does this great truth tie into the truth revealed in verse 8:1?

13

THE SOVEREIGN GRACE OF GOD

Romans Chapter 9

God's eternal purpose is to bless us, and He will. We saw the golden chain of links in Romans Chapter 8: those whom He foreknew, He also predestined; and whom He predestined, these He also called; and whom He called, these He also justified; and whom He justified, these He also glorified.[345] There is no condemnation in Christ,[346] and nothing in the created universe can separate us from His love.[347] God's eternal, unchanging purpose is our good and His glory.

We have seen that God has opened the door and is desiring all to come to Him; "Whoever will call upon the name of the Lord will be saved."[348] Romans emphasizes that the gospel is for all the nations. Romans Chapter 4 looked back to Abraham; "A father of many nations have I made you."[349] Christ said, "Go

---

345 *See* Romans 8:29-30.
346 *See* Romans 8:1
347 *See* Romans 8:39
348 Romans 10:13
349 Romans 4:17, quoting Genesis 17:5. *See also* Genesis 18:18.

therefore and make disciples of all the nations."[350] "For God so loved the world, that He gave His only begotten Son."[351] God's purpose is universal.

But one might ask, what about the nation of Israel? If God's promises to Israel were to fail, God would be untrustworthy. Romans Chapters 9 through 11 address this issue. We will see that God's unchanging purpose is just that – unchangeable. He has not forgotten His people; Israel and the promises of God will be fulfilled. It gives all of us great hope, Jews and Gentiles, to know that "Every word of God is tested; He is a shield to those who take refuge in Him."[352]

Paul's heart – 9:1-5

9:1 *"I am telling the truth in Christ, I am not lying, my conscience bearing me witness in the Holy Spirit,*
9:2 *that I have great sorrow and unceasing grief in my heart.*
9:3 *For I could wish that I myself were accursed, separated from Christ for the sake of my brethren, my kinsmen according to the flesh,*
9:4 *who are Israelites, to whom belongs the adoption as sons and the glory and the covenants and the giving of the Law and the temple service and the promises,*

---

350 Matthew 28:19
351 John 3:16
352 Proverbs 30:5

9:5 *whose are the fathers, and from whom is the Christ according to the flesh, who is over all, God blessed forever. Amen."*

Paul was an Israelite, "circumcised the eighth day, ... of the tribe of Benjamin, a Hebrew of Hebrews."[353] The question of Israel's acceptance of the gospel is a personal issue for him. He writes, "I have great sorrow and unceasing grief in my heart," as he thinks about "his kinsmen according to the flesh."[354] He then makes the shocking statement, "I could wish that I myself were accursed, separated from Christ for the sake of my brethren."[355] This is an amazing characteristic of the apostle Paul. He has a Christ-like, self-sacrificial love for his brothers. James Denney, a Scottish pastor, commenting on Paul's heart in verse 3, called it "a spark from the fire of Christ's substitutionary love." "Greater love has no one than this, that one lay down his life for his friends."[356] Paul's heart is like a spark from that Christ-like fire of substitutionary love.

What a missionary heart Paul has. He writes this knowing, as he wrote at the end of Romans Chapter 8, that nothing can separate us from the love of Christ![357] But He says it here as a solemn oath. Paul has that kind of apostle's (sent one's) heart; he is passionate about it. As believers, we follow one who is the sent One. "In this is love, not that we loved God,

---

353 Philippians 3:5
354 Romans 9:2-3
355 Romans 9:3
356 John 15:13
357 *See* Romans 8:39

but that He loved us and sent His Son."[358] Over thirty times in the gospel of John, Jesus referred to Himself as "sent." If Paul's heart is a spark from the flame of Christ's love, it should cause us to think of the amazing love of God for us in Christ, that He would come to this earth for us.

Has God's word failed? – 9:6-13

9:6 *"But it is not as though the word of God has failed. For they are not all Israel who are descended from Israel;*
9:7 *neither are they all children because they are Abraham's descendants, but: 'Through Isaac your descendants will be named.'*
9:8 *That is, it is not the children of the flesh who are children of God, but the children of the promise are regarded as descendants.*
9:9 *For this is a word of promise: 'At this time I will come, and Sarah shall have a son.'*
9:10 *"And not only this, but there was Rebekah also, when she had conceived twins by one man, our father Isaac;*
9:11 *for though the twins were not yet born, and had not done anything good or bad, in order that God's purpose according to His choice might stand, not because of works, but because of Him who calls,*
9:12 *it was said to her, 'The older will serve the younger.'*
9:13 *Just as it is written, "Jacob I loved, but Esau I hated."'*

Beginning with verse 6, Paul gets back to his task of explaining God's purpose. Thinking of Israel, he asks the question, has

---

358   1 John 4:10

God's word failed? Back in Romans Chapter 2, Paul said that circumcision is not "that which is outward in the flesh," but "that which is of the heart."[359] They are not all Israel who are descended from Israel; rather it is "the children of the promise."[360] Isaac, not Ishmael. God promised to bring the seed through Sarah, not Hagar. "For this is the word of promise: 'At this time I will come, and Sarah shall have a son.'"[361] In verses 10 through 13, Paul goes to another generation. Then Rebecca had twins, and God made a sovereign choice between Jacob and Esau. They had the same mother. God made his choice in the womb before they had done anything. "It was said to her, 'The older will serve the younger.'"[362] This is the opposite of what we would think.

Paul quotes from the prophet Malachi and says, "Just as it is written, 'Jacob I loved, but Esau I hated.'"[363] Christians are sometimes bothered by that language. We need to understand that when God uses the language of "hate," He is speaking of a lesser love. In Matthew, our Lord says, "He who loves father or mother more than Me is not worthy of Me; and he who loves son or daughter more than Me is not worthy of Me."[364] We are familiar with that language from Jesus. In a parallel passage. He puts it this way, "If anyone comes to Me, and does not hate his own father and mother and wife and children and brothers and sisters, yes, and even his own life, he cannot be

---

359 Romans 2:28-29
360 Romans 9:8
361 Romans 9:9
362 Romans 9:12
363 Romans 9:13
364 Matthew 10:37

My disciple."[365] When we come to follow Christ, we become better parents, better children, better husbands, better wives, but our love for Him is to be so supreme that in comparison, lesser loves are called "hate" by Jesus.

Paul is saying in these verses that this is all "in order that God's purpose according to His choice might stand."[366] It is not all Israel who are descended from Israel; it was not Ishmael, but Isaac, the child of promise. He chose not Esau, but Jacob, whose name was changed to Israel, who was chosen before he had done anything right or wrong. Paul answers the question, "Has God's Word failed? No!"

There is no injustice with God – 9:14-18

> **9:14** *"What shall we say then? There is no injustice with God, is there? May it never be!*
> **9:15** *For He says to Moses, 'I will have mercy on whom I have mercy, and I will have compassion on whom I have compassion.'*
> **9:16** *So then it does not depend on the man who wills or the man who runs, but on God who has mercy."*

Paul then addresses another question, is God unjust? Paul answers, "May it never be (*me genoito*)!" "What shall we say then? There is no injustice with God, is there?"[367] He says to Moses, "I will have mercy on whom I have mercy, and I will have

---

365 Luke 14:26
366 Romans 9:11
367 Romans 9:14

compassion on whom I have compassion."[368] If the question is about God's justice, why does Paul bring up mercy? Romans has been teaching us if we received what we deserved, we would all perish! Paul rightfully and logically brings up mercy. Paul quotes from Exodus, where Moses says, Oh Lord "show me your glory!" God answers, "I will be gracious to whom I will be gracious, and will show compassion on whom I will show compassion."[369] It is God's glory to be merciful and compassionate. If we received His justice – "the wages of sin is death!"[370] But God in mercy provided a free gift that cost Him everything. "So it does not depend on the man who wills or the man who runs, but on God who has mercy."[371]

> **9:17** *"For the Scripture says to Pharaoh, 'For this very purpose I raised you up, to demonstrate My power in you, and that My name might be proclaimed throughout the whole earth.'*
> **9:18** *So then He has mercy on whom He desires, and He hardens whom He desires."*

God has demonstrated his glory and mercy. When Moses said, "Show me Your glory," He answered, "Mercy." God raised up Pharaoh, an evil man, a tyrant. We have had many more over the course of history. Moses said to him, "Let My people go." But Moses did not say it that way; he said, "Thus says the Lord, … Let My people go."[372] Pharaoh responds, "Who is the Lord?

---

368 Romans 9:15
369 Exodus 33:18-19
370 Romans 6:23
371 Romans 9:16
372 Exodus 5:1

... I do not know the Lord, and besides, I will not let Israel go."[373] God raised up Pharaoh to show that His purposes will be fulfilled. Pharaoh was judged. He got what he deserved and Israel was spared. Israel got what they did not deserve – mercy. In both cases, it is to God's glory, "That My name might be proclaimed throughout the whole earth."[374]

Why does God still find fault? – 9:19-29

9:19 *"You will say to me then, 'Why does He still find fault? For who resists His will?*

9:20 *On the contrary, who are you, O man, who answers back to God? The thing molded will not say to the molder, 'Why did you make me like this,' will it?"*

To ask the question in verse 19 is to have not read Romans. "Why does He still find fault?"[375] Because we are faulty. We are guilty. The whole race is without excuse. This is the answer to many questions people ask. "Why is there evil in the world?" God is not the author of evil; we are. We are the sinners; He is the merciful one. "Who are you" to answer back to God, Paul says in verse 20. If we have carefully read the gospel, Romans 1:18 through 3:20, man's unrighteousness, the question is not, "Why are some saved and some lost?" The real question is, "Why is anybody saved?" That is the glory of the gospel. If anybody is lost, the blame is theirs. If anybody is saved, the credit is God's.

---

373 Exodus 5:2
374 Romans 9:17
375 Romans 9:19

Paul gives a more extended answer to the question in verses
21 through 23 with the analogy of the right of the potter over
the clay.

> **9:21** *"Or does not the potter have a right over the clay, to
> make from the same lump one vessel for honorable use,
> and another for common use?*
> **9:22** *What if God, although willing to demonstrate His
> wrath and to make His power known, endured with much
> patience vessels of wrath prepared for destruction?*
> **9:23** *And He did so in order that He might make known
> the riches of His glory upon vessels of mercy, which He
> prepared beforehand for glory,"*

People were raising these kinds of questions eight centuries
or so before Christ, and the Lord spoke through His prophet
Isaiah, saying,

> *"Woe to the one who quarrels with his Maker — an earth-
> enware vessel among the vessels of earth! Will the clay
> say to the potter, 'What are you doing?' Or the thing you
> are making say, 'He has no hands?'*

> *Woe to him who says to a father, 'What are you beget-
> ting?' Or to a woman, "To what are you giving birth?'*

> *Thus says the Lord, the Holy One of Israel, and his Maker:
> 'Ask Me about the things to come concerning My sons,
> And you shall commit to Me the work of My hands.*

*It is I who made the earth, and created man upon it. I
stretched out the heavens with My hands And I ordained
all their host."*[376]

God is not at all embarrassed to assert that he is God. He is
the sovereign maker of heaven and earth. Woe to the clay that
would say to the potter, "Why did you make me like this?" Or
complain to his father and mother, "Why are you begetting
me?" God must be allowed to be God. When Paul speaks of the
vessels of mercy, he says, "which He prepared beforehand."[377]
Paul uses the active voice. God takes credit for the vessels of
mercy. The vessels of wrath, on the other hand, Paul says in
the passive voice, were "prepared for destruction."[378] Sin is
man's fault. Romans has taught us the wrath of God rightly falls
on sinners. But mercy is something that God did. He prepared
us as vessels of mercy; there is no merit in us.

God's eternal plan – 9:24-29

9:24 *"even us, whom He also called, not from among Jews
only, but also from among Gentiles.*

9:25 *As He says also in Hosea, 'I will call those who were
not My people, My people,' And her who was not beloved,
'beloved.'*

9:26 *And it shall be that in the place where it was said to
them, 'You are not My people.' There they shall be called
sons of the living God.*

---

376 Isaiah 45:9-12
377 Romans 9:23
378 Romans 9:22

9:27 *And Isaiah cries out concerning Israel, 'Though the number of the sons of Israel be as the sand of the sea, it is the remnant that will be saved;*

9:28 *For the Lord will execute His word upon the earth, thoroughly and quickly.'*

9:29 *And just as Isaiah foretold, 'Except the Lord of Sabaoth had left to us a posterity, we would have become as Sodom, and would have resembled Gomorrah.'"*

Verses 24-29 quotes twice from Hosea and Isaiah,[379] stating that God has always had saving purposes for both Jews and Gentiles. God foreknew all of this. Romans Chapters 9, 10, and 11 are constantly referring to the Old Testament. Paul is laboring to show that the gospel is part of God's eternal plan that He has been writing and acting on throughout history.

What about Israel? – 9:30-33

9:30 *"What shall we say then? That Gentiles, who did not pursue righteousness, attained righteousness, even the righteousness which is by faith;*

9:31 *but Israel, pursuing a law of righteousness, did not arrive at that law.*

9:32 *Why? Because they did not pursue it by faith, but as though it were by works. They stumbled over the stumbling-stone,*

9:33 *just as it is written, 'Behold, I lay in Zion a stone of stumbling and a rock of offense, And he who believes in Him will not be disappointed.'"*

---

379 *See* Hosea 1:10; 2:23 and Isaiah 1:9; 10:22-23

Although Israelites formed the majority of the early church, as you read the book of Acts, you notice the increasing hostility of Israel and their unbelief in the gospel. After Paul's conversion, he was sent to the nations. Yet, in every city to which he would travel, he would first go to the synagogue; "to the Jew first and also to the Greek."[380] Time and again, he would reason from the Scripture in the synagogue with his fellow Jews, and they would cast him out. Paul would then go to the Gentiles. This is the background to Paul raising this issue in verses 30 – 33. Paul says that, by and large, Israel pursued righteousness through law and self-effort. There were exceptions; there were many Jews who became believers. But Israel primarily pursued righteousness through works. The Gentiles, on the other hand, "did not pursue righteousness."[381] Paul has described us, the nations, as having turned away from God and indulging in every kind of sin. Then, by grace, we found that we could be declared righteous in Christ. This is true for Jews or Gentiles. But in verses 30 and 31, Paul says, by and large, Israel did not accept the gospel of Christ because they were busy being self-righteous and trying to attain righteousness on their own. They did not pursue righteousness by faith, but by works and "they stumbled over the stumbling-stone."[382] Paul writes in 1 Corinthians:

> *"For Indeed Jews ask for signs and Greeks search for wisdom; but we preach Christ crucified, to Jews a stumbling block and to Gentiles foolishness, but to those who*

---

380 Romans 1:16
381 Romans 9:30
382 Romans 9:32

are the called, both Jews and Greeks, Christ the power
of God and the wisdom of God."[383]

I remember the first Jewish man that I witnessed to personally; although I do not know if he was actually the first Jewish person because it is not my habit to ask someone, are you Jew or Gentile? This was when I was attending the university and I knew he was Jewish because his nickname was "Rabbi." This may not have been an appropriate nickname, but he took it in good humor. We were friends. I began to tell him about Jesus, and he was interested. He asked questions and we got together several times. I bought him a Bible with a New Testament in it. I said, "Let me show you how the New Testament fulfills the Old Testament." I have never forgotten the times we had because I would show him in the New Testament the Hebrew Scripture where it would say, "So that what was spoken through the prophets might be fulfilled."[384] He was intrigued. I used the book of Matthew quite a bit because Matthew is very Jewish. I read, "The virgin will be with child ... and they will call His name, Immanuel" — God with us.[385] My friend's face fell and he said, "That's my stumbling block." I told him, "Did you know the Bible said you would say that?" We turned to Romans 9:32-33, "They stumbled over the stumbling stone, just as it is written, Behold I lay in Zion a stone of stumbling and a rock of offense and he who believes in Him will not be disappointed." It is sad and tragic to see anyone stumble over Jesus Christ and Him crucified, whether he be Jew or Gentile.

---

383 1 Corinthians 1:22-23
384 *See e.g., Matthew 2:23; Matthew 13:35; Matthew 21:4*
385 Matthew 1:23

Romans Chapter 9 can be summarized by looking at two questions. The first, verses 6 — 29, "Why is anybody saved?" We are sinful; our minds are depraved; "There is none who seeks for God,"[386] not even one. If anyone is saved, it is because of God's sovereign election and mercy. The second question, verses 30 — 33, is, "Why is anyone lost?" We are lost because of our unbelief; our stubborn refusal to believe in the One who says, "Come to Me, so that you may have life."[387]

God's sovereignty and man's responsibility

If Romans Chapter 9 emphasizes God's sovereignty, Chapter 10 represents man's responsibility. "Whoever will call upon the name of the Lord will be saved."[388] Paul does not try to harmonize these two things. The Bible teaches that God is absolutely sovereign and the Bible teaches that man is responsible for his own sin. The Bible also says that God is not willing that any should perish. Many Christians try to harmonize these two principles; often dividing into different camps choosing one or the other because we cannot fully put them together. Let the two stand side-by-side; God's sovereign grace of election and God's love poured out through Jesus Christ to all who will believe. The Bible often sets these two principles side by side.

For example, in Matthew 11, these two truths that flow out of Romans are side by side in the scene where our Lord Jesus says, "Come to me, all who are weary and heavy laden."[389]

---

386 Romans 3:11
387 John 5:40. *See also* John 10:10; 17:2
388 Romans 10:13
389 Matthew 11:28

The sinfulness of our mind and soul is so serious that we do not seek Him; He had to seek us. Sin is so devastating that it turns us completely away from the Lord.

> *"Jesus answered and said, 'I praise You, O Father, Lord of heaven and earth, that You have hidden these things from the wise and intelligent and have revealed them to babes.*
>
> *Yes, Father, for this was well-pleasing in Your sight.*
>
> *All things have been handed over to Me by My Father; and no one knows the Son except the Father; nor does anyone know the Father except the Son, and anyone to whom the Son wills to reveal Him.*
>
> *'Come to Me, all who are weary and heavy-laden, and I will give you rest."*
>
> *Take My yoke upon you and learn from Me, for I am gentle and humble in heart, and you will find rest for your souls.*
>
> *For My yoke is easy and My load is light."*[390]

In verse 25 Jesus burst into praise. Luke also records this scene in Chapter 10 where the added detail is given that Jesus, "Rejoiced greatly in the Holy Spirit."[391]

---

390 Matthew 11:25-30
391 Luke 10:21

Jesus praised the Lord for His sovereignty. He rejoiced greatly in the Holy Spirit. Side by side to that truth is the truth in Matthew 11:28, "Come to me all who are weary and are heavy laden." If you are tired and burdened by your sin, come to the Savior. If you are weary and heavy laden you will find rest for your soul. You have on the one hand, Jesus bursting into praise, thinking of the sovereign grace of God expressed in Romans 9. "It does not depend on the man who wills or the man who runs, but on God who has mercy."[392] At the same time, Jesus is saying in Romans 10, "Whoever will call upon the name of the Lord will be saved."[393] Come to Me, "you will find rest for your souls."[394]

Paul's response to writing about God's sovereign grace and man's responsibility in Romans Chapters 9 and 10 is to put his pen down, in effect, at the end of Chapter 11 and say, "Oh the depth of the riches both of the wisdom and knowledge of God! How unsearchable are His judgments and unfathomable His ways! … who became His counselor? … For from Him and through Him and to Him are all things. To Him be the glory forever."[395] Paul concludes by worshiping God. That is the proper response.

---

392 Romans 9:16
393 Romans 10:13
394 Matthew 11:29
395 Romans 11:33-36

Study question

- What can we learn from the example of Paul's heart for his kinsmen shown in verses 9:1–5?

- How does Paul's explanation of Israel being "children of the promise" answer the question of whether God's word, His promises, to Israel have somehow failed (9:6-13)?

- How would you respond to the argument that the exercise of God's sovereignty somehow makes Him unjust?

- What is the "stone of stumbling" referred to by Paul in verse 9:33?

- What is the relationship between God's sovereignty and our responsibility to believe in Christ?

14

THE GREAT CALL OF THE GOSPEL

Romans Chapters 10 — 11

We are entering a beautiful chapter where, right in the middle of Romans Chapters 9 to 11, there is a sweeping summary of God's eternal purposes. We previously looked at the emphasis in Romans Chapter 9 of the Sovereign Grace of God. Here in Chapter 10, Paul writes of the great call of the gospel to anyone and everyone. As I said, we should leave those two truths to stand side by side. Christians often struggle with that. Those who grasp the sovereign grace of God often exclude the "universal call of the gospel." Those of us who are captured by the love of the universal gospel, of whoever will call on the name of the Lord, sometimes are not comfortable with the fact that God chose us. Churches sometimes divide over that. We should embrace both truths as the Bible presents them side by side; Romans 9 and Romans 10.

Zeal without knowledge – 10:1-4

10:1 *"Brethren, my heart's desire and my prayer to God for them is for their salvation.*

10:2 *For I bear them witness that they have a zeal for God, but not in accordance with knowledge.*

10:3 *For not knowing about God's righteousness, and seeking to establish their own, they did not subject themselves to the righteousness of God.*

10:4 *For Christ is the end of the law for righteousness to everyone who believes."*

Paul is heartbroken. His countrymen had zeal, they were sincere, but their zeal was "not in accordance with knowledge."[396] Israel sought to establish its own way rather than submit to God. Many self-willed, stubborn people fit this category. They think they can establish their own righteousness and come into God's presence with their own effort. It is popular to think, "As long as you are sincere in your belief, you will be OK." This describes many religious people. Having zeal without real knowledge of the cross of Christ and why it is necessary is a dangerous combination. When you get on an airplane, you do not want the pilot to climb into the cockpit and say, "I have never flown a plane, but I am really sincere. I will try hard to do my best." You want the pilot to know how to fly that plane. Zeal, without knowledge, is dangerous in many areas of life.

I was rebuilding the deck on my house and was going to detach a stairway and move it. I looked it over and I thought I could do it. My dad happened to be there helping me, and he said,

---

396 Romans 10:2

"I think that's too heavy. If you detach it, I think you're going to find it heavier than you think." I looked at it again and said, "No I can do it." My dad said, "No, let's put a brace on it so that when we detach it, it won't crush you." I was sure it was not that heavy but I thought, "He's my dad." Honor your father and mother. Obey your parents. So, we put a brace under it. My dad saved my life. The stairway was so heavy that the brace barely held it. It would have crushed me. Sincerity is not enough. If that is true with airplanes and carpentry and all areas of life, how much more is it true with our eternal relationship with our Creator.

Righteousness based on Law – 10:5

10:5 *"For Moses writes that the man who practices the righteousness which is based on law shall live by that righteousness."*

"Moses writes" (which is to say, "the Law says") regarding "the righteousness which is based on Law;" that the man who practices these things shall live by them.[397] Paul is quoting Leviticus 18, a man may live if he does (if he keeps) God's statutes.[398] If righteousness were able to be obtained by the Law, you must live by that law, and you must do it perfectly. Paul quotes that in Galatians Chapter 3, "However, the Law is not of faith; on the contrary, 'He who practices them shall live by them.'"[399] "For as many as are of the works of the Law

---

397 Romans 10:**5**
398 Leviticus 18:5
399 Galatians 3:12

are under a curse; for it is written, 'Cursed is everyone who does not abide by all things written in the book of the Law, to perform them.'"[400]

Jesus said the same thing. A man came up to Him and asked, "Good Teacher, what should I do to inherit eternal life?"[401] Jesus answered,

> *"Why do you call Me good? No one is good except God alone. You know the commandments, Do not murder, Do not commit adultery, Do not steal, Do not bear false witness, Do not defraud, Honor your father and mother."*[402]

Jesus had just said, "No one is good but God;" He then gave him the latter half of the commandments, the ones that are horizontal — toward one another. The man responded,

> *"'Teacher, I have kept all these things from my youth up." And looking at him, Jesus felt a love for him, and said, 'One thing you lack: go and sell all you possess, and give it to the poor, and you will have treasure in heaven; and come, follow Me.'"*[403]

In saying that, Jesus turned to the first half of the commandments about loving God with everything you have. Jesus said, OK, turn loose of your possessions and follow me. "At these words [the man's] face fell, and he went away grieved, for he

---

400 Galatians 3:10
401 Mark 10:17
402 Mark 10:18-19
403 Mark 10:20-21

was one who owned much property."[404] He did not keep the first commandment; he had another god besides God. "You cannot serve God and mammon (money).[405] Jesus had touched on his heart condition, and the man went away grieved. Yes, he "owned much property," but as someone has well said, "much property owned him."

Righteousness based on Law speaks that way. Religious people need to hear this. I ministered for four years in Salt Lake City, Utah, which is the headquarters of Mormonism (The Church of Jesus Christ of the Latter-Day Saints). They are very zealous people but not subject to the righteousness of God in Christ. I was invited to the office of one of their highest officials to talk about these things. They are busy working on their righteousness as if it is by Law and works. I quoted Galatians 3:10 and James Chapter 2:10, "Whoever keeps the whole law and yet stumbles in one point, he has become guilty of all." The official said to me, "That's not in the Bible." I said, "Yes, it is." He became angry and was unable to accept what I was saying.

Righteousness based on faith – 10:6-8

> **10:6** *"But the righteousness based on faith speaks thus, 'Do not say in your heart, Who will ascend into heaven?' (that is, to bring Christ down).*
> **10:7** *or, 'Who will descend into the abyss?' (that is, to bring Christ up from the dead).*

---

404 Mark 10:22
405 Matthew 6:24

10:8 *But what does it say? 'The Word is near you, in your mouth and in your heart' — that is, the word of faith which we are preaching,*

10:9 *that If you confess with your mouth Jesus as Lord, and believe in your heart that God raised Him from the dead, you will be saved;*

10:10 *for with the heart man believes, resulting in righteousness, and with the mouth he confesses, resulting in salvation."*

In contrast to the righteousness based on Law, Paul quotes Deuteronomy 30 and says that "righteousness is based on faith."[406] This is the righteousness of Romans. There is nothing left for us to do — God has done it. Jesus Christ came, bore our sins on the cross,[407] and He has ascended to heaven. The word of faith that Paul proclaimed "is near you,"[408] all you have to do is believe.

Verse 9 reiterates the simplicity of the gospel. It is not what we do; it is what Jesus Christ did. We announce this good news. It is finished. He died, He was buried, He rose again. He is seated at the right hand of the Father. "Believe in your heart" and "confess with your mouth" that He is Lord and you will be saved.[409] Paul explains that with the heart, man believes resulting in righteousness, and with the mouth, he confesses resulting in salvation. If there is belief in the heart, there will be confession with the mouth. Jesus said what comes out of

---

406 *See* Romans 10:6
407 *See* 1 Peter 2:24
408 Romans 10:8
409 Romans 10:9

the mouth comes from the heart.[410] There are some people who try to be secret believers who do not say anything about their faith. But Romans 10:10 instructs us to confess that Jesus is Lord. Believe in your heart that God raised Him from the dead and confess with your mouth that He is Lord.

The gospel is available to all – 10:11-13

10:11 *"For the Scripture says, 'Whoever believes in Him will not be disappointed.'*

10:12 *For there is no distinction between Jew and Greek; for the same Lord is Lord of all, abounding in riches for all who call upon Him;*

10:13 *for 'Whoever will call upon the name of the Lord will be saved."*

The gospel is for "whoever will call on the name of the Lord;"[411] whoever will believe in Him. There is no distinction between Jew and Gentile. Christ died for all. God so loved the world that whoever will call on his name will be saved.[412] He abounds in riches; He is rich in mercy for whoever will call out to Him.[413]

Sharing the gospel – 10:14-15

10:14 *"How then will they call upon Him in whom they have not believed? And how will they believe in Him whom they have not heard? And how will they hear without a preacher?*

---

410 *See* Matthew 12:34
411 Romans 10:13
412 *See* Romans 10:13
413 *See* Ephesians 2:4

10:15 *And how will they preach unless they are sent? Just as it is written, 'How beautiful are the feet of those who bring glad tidings of good things.'"*

As soon as we come to know Jesus Christ, we have a desire for others to know Him. Our Lord Jesus mandated that saying, "Go therefore and make disciples of all the nations."[414] "As the Father sent Me, I also send you."[415] Paul asks, "How then will they call upon Him in whom they have not believed? And how will they believe [if] they have not heard?" Because faith comes from hearing. "And how will they hear" if we do not proclaim?[416] And then, "How will they preach unless they are sent?"[417] All of us are to be involved in gospel proclamation. Some of us are called to be out in front and preach. Others are to be behind the scenes, sending, praying, and giving. But it is the responsibility of every believer to proclaim this good news.

It is a beautiful thing to be representing Jesus Christ to our generation. It is a beautiful thing in God's sight when we take our feet and use them to bring the good news.[418] Paul is quoting Chapter 52 of Isaiah,[419] which comes right before the great 53rd chapter; that amazing prophecy of the Lamb of God who would lay down his life for us and take it up again; "the man of sorrows ... acquainted with grief."[420] Isaiah also writes how

---

414   Matthew 28:19
415   John 20:21
416   Romans 10:14
417   Romans 10:15
418   *Id.*
419   *See* Isaiah 52:7
420   Isaiah 53:3

"all of us like sheep have gone astray, each of us has turned to his own way."[421] This sounds a lot like Romans: "There is none righteous, not even one;"[422] "all have sinned and fall short of the glory of God."[423] The Lord has caused the iniquity of us all to fall on Him, to fall on another. This is the core of the gospel. How beautiful are the feet of those who bring this good news.

Israel's rejection – 10:16-21

10:16 *"However, they did not all heed the glad tidings; for Isaiah says, 'Lord, who has believed our report?'*

10:17 *So faith comes from hearing, and hearing by the word of Christ.*

10:18 *But I say, surely they have never heard, have they? Indeed they have: 'Their voice has gone out into all the earth, And their words to the ends of the world.'*

10:19 *But I say, surely Israel did not know, did they? At the first Moses says, 'I will make you jealous by that which is not a nation, by a nation without understanding will I anger you.'*

10:20 *And Isaiah is very bold and says, 'I was found by those who sought Me not, I became manifest to those who did not ask for Me.'*

10:21 *But as for Israel He says, 'All the day long I have stretched out My hands to a disobedient and obstinate people.'"*

---

421 Isaiah 53:6
422 Romans 3:10
423 Romans 3:23

Jesus was rejected. His message was rejected. But rejection, even by Israel, does not mean there is a problem with the message. We are called to preach the word and to proclaim His Son, whether people want to hear it or not. Paul told Timothy, there will come a time when they will not want to hear, but you must be faithful to preach the word.[424] For "faith comes from hearing, and hearing by the word of Christ."[425] You and I have the great privilege of proclaiming the gospel. The righteous man lives by faith, taking God at His word. That is why I am so passionate about proclaiming not my words but His Word, the Scripture itself.

Even after this clarion call to missionary activity, Paul does not excuse Israel's or Gentile's unbelief. Everyone is responsible before God. He writes in verse 18, "I say, surely they have never heard, have they? Indeed, they have: 'Their voice has gone out into all the earth, And their words to the ends of the world.'"[426] Paul is quoting from the 19th Psalm, "The heavens are telling of the glory of God; ... Day to day pours forth speech."[427] Since the creation of the world, God has been known. Paul has come full circle. In Romans Chapter 1, he wrote, "For since the creation of the world His invisible attributes, His eternal power and divine nature, have been clearly seen, ... For even though they knew God, they did not honor Him as God or give [Him] thanks."[428] We are all without excuse for not believing in God. The creation itself is His testimony, and Israel is without

424 *See* 2 Timothy 4:2
425 Roman 10:17
426 Romans 10:18
427 Psalm 19:1-2
428 Romans 1:20-21

THE GREAT CALL OF THE GOSPEL · **197**

excuse. Romans is written by a heartbroken Jew, and he quotes the Old Testament in the last verse saying, "All the day long I stretched out my hands to a disobedient and obstinate people."[429] This is the heart of God.

Is Israel's rejection total? – 11:1-10

There are two great questions that Paul addresses in Romans Chapter 11, and both of them flow out of Chapters 9 and 10. The first question, verse 1, is Israel's rejection total? And the second question, verse 11, is Israel's rejection of the gospel final? Did Israel totally reject the gospel, and will Israel always and finally reject the gospel? Both times Paul raises the questions, he answers with the emphatic, *"Me genoito"* (may it never be)!

> **11:1** *"I say then, God has not rejected His people, has He? May it never be! For I too am an Israelite, a descendant of Abraham, of the tribe of Benjamin.*
> **11:2** *God has not rejected His people whom He foreknew. Or do you not know what the Scripture says in the passage about Elijah, how he pleads with God against Israel?*
> **11:3** *'Lord, they have killed Your prophets, they have torn down Your altars, and I alone am left, and they are seeking my life.'*
> **11:4** *But what is the divine response to him? 'I have kept for Myself seven thousand men who have not bowed the knee to Baal.'*

---

429 Romans 10:21

11:5 *In the same way then, there has also come to be at the present time a remnant according to God's gracious choice.*

11:6 *But it is by grace, it is no longer on the basis of works, otherwise grace is no longer grace.*

11:7 *What then? That which Israel is seeking for, it has not obtained, but those who were chosen obtained it, and the rest were hardened;*

11:8 *just as it is written, 'God gave them a spirit of stupor, eyes to see not and ears to hear not, down to this very day.'*

11:9 *And David says, 'Let their table become a snare and a trap, and a stumbling block and a retribution to them.*

11:10 *'Let their eyes be darkened to see not, and bend their backs forever.'"*

I am a Jew, Paul says, "an Israelite, a descendant of Abraham."[430] The first believers were Jews. The early church was full of Israelites. Although it might seem like most of Israel was in unbelief, Paul says, "No, Israel's rejection is not total." It was just like in Elijah's day. Elijah felt alone, outnumbered by the prophets of Baal. Even after the great showdown when God showed Himself powerful, Elijah was discouraged and said, "I alone am left."[431] Jezebel was seeking his life. But the Lord said, "I have kept for myself seven thousand men who have not bowed their knee to Baal."[432] God is always at work, and He has His remnant according to His gracious choice.[433] It was not a total rejection of Israel. Three thousand Israelites had

430 Romans 11:1
431 Romans 11:3, quoting 1 King 19:10
432 Romans 11:4, citing 1 King 19:18
433 *See* Romans 11:5

believed on Pentecost, and by Acts Chapter 4, there were at least five thousand men.[434] Paul answers his own question, "Has God totally rejected His people?" "May it never be."[435]

Was Israel's rejection final? – 11:11-16

11:11 *"I say then, they did not stumble so as to fall, did they? May it never be! But by their transgression salvation has come to the Gentiles, to make them jealous.*

11:12 *Now if their transgression be riches for the world and their failure be riches for the Gentiles, how much more will their fulfillment be!*

11:13 *But I am speaking to you who are Gentiles. Inasmuch then as I am an apostle of Gentiles, I magnify my ministry,*
11:14 *if somehow I might move to jealousy my fellow countrymen and save some of them.*

11:15 *For if their rejection be the reconciliation of the world, what will their acceptance be but life from the dead?*

11:16 *And if the first piece of dough be holy, the lump is also; and if the root be holy, the branches are too.*

The state of affairs that Paul was addressing in his day was Israel rejecting the gospel. It was being embraced by the Gentiles. God would use that to provoke Jewish jealousy. This is true even today. But if Israel's rejection brought riches to the world, Paul says, how much more will their final belief bring blessing?[436] Is the state of unbelief that Israel is in nationally

---

434 Acts 4:4
435 Romans 11:1
436 Romans 11:12

her final condition? Did Israel "stumble so as to fall [to ruin]?" "May it never be!"[437] That is the second half of Chapter 11. There is a future for Israel. God is going to fulfill His promises. Israel's rejection is not final.

Analogy of the olive tree – *11:17-24*

In the following verses, Paul gives an extended analogy of the olive tree, an illustration of the place of God's blessing in the sweep of history. Paul is explaining God's unthwartable purposes. You do not have to understand every detail to rejoice that God is at work

> **11:17** *"But if some of the branches were broken off, and you, being a wild olive, were grafted in among them and became partaker with them of the rich root of the olive tree,*
> **11:18** *do not be arrogant toward the branches; but if you are arrogant, remember that it is not you who supports the root, but the root supports you.*
> **11:19** *You will say then, 'Branches were broken off so that I might be grafted in.'*
> **11:20** *Quite right, they were broken off for their unbelief, and you stand only by your faith. Do not be conceited, but fear;*
> **11:21** *for if God did not spare the natural branches, neither will He spare you.*
> **11:22** *Behold then the kindness and severity of God; to those who fell, severity, but to you, God's kindness, if you continue in His kindness; otherwise you also will be cut off.*

437 Romans 11:11

11:23 *And they also, if they do not continue in their unbelief, will be grafted in; for God is able to graft them in again.*
11:24 *For if you were cut off from what is by nature a wild olive tree, and were grafted contrary to nature into a cultivated olive tree, how much more shall these who are the natural branches be grafted into their own olive tree?"*

Paul is speaking to Gentiles, which includes most of us (anyone who is not Jewish). In saying this, it is important to note that "there is no distinction between Jew and Greek (Gentile);"[438] there are no racial or ethnic distinctions within the church. "There is neither Jew nor Greek, there is neither slave nor free man, there is neither male nor female."[439] It seems best to understand this as a general statement of warning to "Gentiles" who might be tempted to take the blessing of the gospel lightly. He is not, as such, addressing individual believers, but rather the general mindset that Gentiles might fall into (and indeed have fallen into). Paul is addressing the fact that there are many more Gentiles in the church than Jews and, by and large, the Jews have rejected their Savior. Paul gives two warnings to those of us who are Gentiles. First, we should beware of becoming proud or arrogant. Do not be proud that we are in God's family and Israel has been rejected. "Do not be arrogant toward the branches; but if you are arrogant, remember that it is not you who supports the root, but the root supports you."[440]

---

438 Romans 10:12
439 Galatians 3:28
440 Romans 11:18

202 · A BRIEF EXPOSITION OF ROMANS

Israel's unbelief has opened the door to all the nations, all the peoples of the earth, finding salvation. You may say, "branches were broken off that I may be grafted in. Quite right, they were broken off for their unbelief and you stand only by your faith." [441] Paul says, do not be arrogant or conceited, but reverently fear.[442] Paul is not speaking here of individuals being broken off, he is speaking of the blessing of God on a nation. The nation of Israel was broken off because of its unbelief. And speaking to the nations, all of us, we stand because of faith; we have laid hold of Christ by faith.

Second, Paul warns if God did not spare the natural branch, He will not spare us if we turn away in unbelief. Sadly, there are places in our world where whole nations have turned away from the gospel truth they once had. There is not much openness to Christianity in Europe today. A coldness has set in where the gospel once bore much fruit, and so many were blessed. This same coldness is currently setting in throughout the United States. Fewer and fewer people are responsive to the gospel. If God broke off Israel from the place of blessing because of their unbelief, we Gentile nations should be careful of being arrogant.

All Israel will be saved – 11:25-32

> **11:25** *"For I do not want you, brethren, to be uninformed of this mystery, lest you be wise in your own estimation,*

---

441 Romans 11:19-20
442 *See* Romans 11:20

that a partial hardening has happened to Israel until the
fullness of the Gentiles has come in;
11:26 *and thus all Israel will be saved; just as it is written,*
'The Deliverer will come from Zion, He will remove ungod-
liness from Jacob.'
11:27 *'And this is My covenant with them, when I take*
away their sins.'
11:28 *From the standpoint of the gospel they are enemies*
for your sake, but from the standpoint of God's choice they
are beloved for the sake of the fathers;
11:29 *for the gifts and the calling of God are irrevocable.*
11:30 *For just as you once were disobedient to God but*
now have been shown mercy because of their disobedience,
11:31 *so these also now have been disobedient, in order*
that because of the mercy shown to you they also may
now be shown mercy.
11:32 *For God has shut up all in disobedience that He*
might show mercy to all."

In the sweep of God's unshakeable purpose, Israel has had "a partial hardening." In God's good timing, when "the fullness of the Gentiles [of all the nations] have come in,"[443] God will bring Israel back into a state of belief. When God wraps up history, when the Alpha and the Omega finish the story, "all Israel will be saved."[444] "The Deliverer will come from Zion, [and] He will remove ungodliness from Jacob [Israel]."[445] I believe that this will be fulfilled as He purges out the unbelief

---

443 Romans 11:25
444 Romans 11:26
445 *Id.*

as revealed in the Book of Revelation. Chapter 1 of Revelation references Zechariah, "Every eye will see Him, even those who pierced Him; and all the tribes of the earth will mourn over Him."[446] The rejection of Israel is not final. There will be a future recognition of the only Savior, Jesus Christ. There will be conversion, and it will be through faith because faith is always the way that a righteous man lives.

Paul has written much in these verses, and we often struggle with all that he is saying. But essentially, he is underlining that God's promises will not fail. This great gospel that Paul proclaims will not negate God's promises to Israel. One day soon, there will be people of every tribe and tongue praising God.

To summarize what has been said in Romans so far, "God has shut up all in disobedience that He might show mercy to all."[447] Man is sinful and disobedient; God is merciful. Paul has taught through the whole gospel: the gracious choice of God; the wickedness of men and the provision of Jesus Christ; the universal call, "whoever will call on the name of the Lord will be saved."[448] God will see to it that none of His promises fail.

Paul's worship – 11:33-36

> **11:33** *"Oh, the depth of the riches both of the wisdom and knowledge of God! How unsearchable are His judgments and unfathomable His ways!*

---

446 Revelation 1:7, cf. Zechariah 12:10
447 Romans 11:32
448 Romans 10:13

11:34 *For who has known the mind of the Lord, or who became His counselor?*

11:35 *Or who has first given to Him that it might be paid back to Him again?*

11:36 *For from Him and through Him and to Him are all things. To Him be the glory forever. Amen."*

At the end of Chapter 11, Paul bursts into worship. This is the proper response to God's grace. You will never put God in your debt. No one, Jew, Gentile, male, female, religious, irreligious, will ever be able to say, "God owes me something." God in his great wisdom and love has provided us salvation, but it comes entirely from His grace.

Study questions

- Why was Israel's "zeal for God" insufficient?

- How does righteousness based on faith differ from righteousness based on law?

- What must we do to be saved according to verse 10:9?

- If God has been known to all the earth, why is it still important for us to proclaim the gospel?

- What does the analogy of the olive tree in 11:17-24 tell us about the relationship between Israel and the Gentiles?

- What does Romans 11 say about Israel's rejection of Christ and God's plan for His people?

15

PRACTICAL RIGHTEOUSNESS

Romans 12

The great responsibility of every person is to worship God. Romans begins by saying we refuse to honor God as God. But we have seen the great unfolding of the salvation that Romans presents. We have enjoyed that the righteous God of the universe has provided a righteousness for us in His Son. After explaining this for eleven chapters, Paul bursts into worship — the final paragraph of Chapter 11.

After eleven chapters, we now come to the first real exhortation in Romans. What should our response be? This is the pattern all the way through the Bible: truth then response — the application of the truth. Doctrine then duty. It is easy to get that backward. The principle of doctrine first is not only logical, it is liberating. The balance of Romans, from 12:1 to the end, is presenting our duties, our right response to the salvation He has given us. We who have been declared righteous should live a life characterized by practical righteousness. Our righteous standing should result in righteous living day by day.

Practical righteousness in relationship to God – 12:1-2

12:1 *"I urge you therefore, brethren, by the mercies of God, to present your bodies a living and holy sacrifice, acceptable to God, which is your spiritual service of worship.* **12:2** *And do not be conformed to this world, but be transformed by the renewing of your mind, that you may prove what the will of God is, that which is good and acceptable and perfect."*

What should our response be? We are to present ourselves to Him. Even here, Paul does not command it, he urges it. He uses the verbal form of the word "urge," which is also used to describe the Holy Spirit, the Encourager. God wants us to be overwhelmed by His grace, and Paul encourages us to present ourselves to Him. He says, "I urge you ... by the mercies of God." That is a simple way to describe all that God has done for us. Christ died in our place. God was rich in mercy.[449] We deserve death; we have life. We deserve condemnation, but He declared us right with Him.

When Paul says we are "to present [our] bodies a living and holy sacrifice," he is saying we should give Him everything. You are not your own; you have been bought with a price. We should give ourselves without reservation to Him. We should abandon ourselves to Him. You can trust Him fully; He is for you.[450] Sometimes I ask myself; would I be willing to die for Jesus? So far, He has not asked me to. He has

---

449 *See* Ephesians 2:4
450 *See* Romans 8:31

asked me to live for Him. "Present your bodies a living and holy sacrifice." We are to be completely devoted to Him, everything we have; our time, our energies, our money, everything. When Paul uses this language of sacrifice, it brings to my mind an altar where we present ourselves to Him.

Paul writes in 2 Corinthians,

> *"For the love of Christ controls us, having concluded this, that one died for all, therefore all died; and He died for all, that they who live should no longer live for themselves, but for Him who died and rose again on their behalf."*[451]

You can see the logic behind what Paul is saying. The great love of Christ for us should control us. If we have realized that He died for us and that we died with Him, we can now live a new life completely given over to Him. This is not only pleasing to God, it is our "spiritual service of worship."[452] It is the only rational thing to do. If God gave his Son for me, I should give my life for Him, and Paul urges us to do just that.

Verse 2 describes what it will look like to be given over to Him. We are not to be conformed to this world, not like all those around us who do not know Him. We are not to be conformed to the culture around us; to those who are self-seeking and self-centered. We should not externally give in to a world

---

451   2 Corinthians 5:14-15
452   Romans 12:1

that rejects Christ. "Do not be conformed to this world, but be transformed."[453] This is to be changed from the inside out. He wants us to be completely new, with new attitudes, new values, new priorities, and a new mindset. "If anyone is in Christ, he is a new creature; the old things passed away; behold, new things have come."[454]

We are to be transformed. This term is only used four times in the New Testament. Twice it is used of Jesus when He took Peter, James, and John with Him up on the mountain "and He was transfigured before them.[455]" His appearance changed. They could barely describe it. It was a complete transformation as He unveiled a bit of His glory. The other time it is used is in 2 Corinthians 3, "We all, with unveiled face, beholding as in a mirror the glory of the Lord, are being transformed into the same image from glory to glory, just as from the Lord, the Spirit."[456] This is a great description of what Paul is saying in Romans 12. He wants us to be transformed by the renewing of our minds, the way we think.

Before we come to Christ, we have a depraved mind. That is where Romans 1 starts. Wrong thinking man did not want to thank God; did not want to worship God, and God gave him over to a depraved mind. But when you come to Christ, you see everything new. Paul wants to build on that process of growth as we start to learn how to think His thoughts. Paul

---

453 Romans 12:2
454 2 Corinthians 5:17
455 Matthew 17:2
456 2 Corinthians 3:18

further describes this process in 2 Corinthians. Before we come to Christ, he says,

> *"If our gospel is veiled, it is veiled to those who are perishing, in whose case the god of this world [Satan] has blinded the minds of the unbelieving, that they might not see the light of the gospel of the glory of Christ, who is the image of God."*[457]

"But whenever a person turns to the Lord, the veil is taken away"[458] to see who He really is. "Now the Lord is the Spirit, and where the Spirit of the Lord is, there is liberty (freedom)."[459] You are then born and begin to grow and be transformed as you renew your mind. With an unveiled face, we behold "as in a mirror the glory of the Lord."[460]

James says that the Bible is the mirror.[461] It is the Word of God. As you look into the Bible, you see the beauty of Christ. The Holy Spirit wants us to see Jesus, not like a forgetful hearer but an effectual doer of the Word.[462] As we spend time in God's Word, looking at His Son, He transforms us into the image of Jesus. It is God's purpose that we become more and more Christlike. That is the Holy Spirit's ministry, and it is an ongoing process from "glory to glory"[463] as we renew our minds.

---

457 2 Corinthians 4:3-4
458 2 Corinthians 3:16
459 2 Corinthians 3:17
460 2 Corinthians 3:18
461 *See* James 1:23-25
462 *See* James 1:25
463 2 Corinthians 3:18

We need to transform the thinking in our minds and hearts daily. That is why the very first song in the songbook (Psalms) says,

> "How blessed is the man who does not walk in the counsel of the wicked (who does not get his input from this world), ... but his delight is in the law (the Word) of the Lord, And in His law he meditates day and night."[464]

This is practical righteousness in relationship to God. God is well pleased when we present ourselves to Him daily and allow Him to have charge of our life, particularly regarding the gifts God has given to each one of us.

Practical righteousness in relationship to ourselves – 12:3-8

12:3 *"For through the grace given to me I say to every man among you not to think more highly of himself than he ought to think; but to think so as to have sound judgment, as God has allotted to each a measure of faith.*

12:4 *For just as we have many members in one body and all the members do not have the same function,*

12:5 *so we, who are many, are one body in Christ, and individually members one of another.*

12:6 *And since we have gifts that differ according to the grace given to us, let each exercise them accordingly: if prophecy, according to the proportion of his faith;*

464 Psalms 1:1-2

12:7 *if service, in his serving; or he who teaches, in his teaching;*
12:8 *or he who exhorts, in his exhortation; he who gives, with liberality; he who leads, with diligence; he who shows mercy, with cheerfulness."*

Paul starts this section by saying, do not think too highly of yourself.[465] This is a sober assessment that we often ignore. Paul will emphasize this point again in verse 16, "Do not be haughty in mind, but associate with the lowly. Do not be wise in your own estimation." This is very much part of our natural way of thinking. We are self-absorbed and proud. The gospel humbles us. A renewed mind is a humble mind.

He then introduces the analogy of the body. We are the body of Christ, members of one another, and we each have different gifts. The Bible uses a number of analogies for the Church: the bride, the building, the flock, but comparing the church to a human is perhaps the most common. In 1 Corinthians, for example, Paul writes, "For even as the body is one and yet has many members, and all the members of the body, though they are many, are one body, so also is Christ."[466] Just as the human body is a marvel of diversity and yet unity, "so we, who are many, are one body in Christ, and individually members one of another."[467]

---

465   *See* Romans 12:3
466   1 Corinthians 12:12
467   Romans 12:5

214 • A BRIEF EXPOSITION OF ROMANS

There are four places in the New Testament where we are told that everyone born again into Christ is given a special gift. No two of us are alike. The gifts of the Holy Spirit are taught here in Romans 12, 1 Corinthians 12, Ephesians 4, and 1 Peter 4.[468] Peter broadly categorizes between speaking gifts and serving gifts and says, "As each one has received a special gift, employ it in serving one another as good stewards of God's manifold grace."[469] If you have a speaking gift (and Romans 12 mentions a few here: prophecy, teaching, exhorting), Peter says, speak "as one who is speaking the utterances of God."[470] If you have a serving gift, serve "by the strength which God supplies."[471] That is a good summary of what Paul is saying here in verses 3 through 8.

We should not depreciate the spiritual gift we have been given. Every Christian is gifted, and we are to exercise our gift to the mutual building up of the body of Christ. Some Christians wish for a different gift; "I wish I could sing like she can sing," or "I wish I could teach the way he can teach." God has gifted each of us for a particular role in the body of Christ. He has made us how we are, and He knows how He has gifted us. But neither should we think too highly of our gift. It is a gift from God; it is not ours. We should exercise it and use it for God's glory.

---

468 *See* 1 Corinthians 12:4-12; Ephesians 4:13-16; 1 Peter 4:10-11.
469 1 Peter 4:10
470 1 Peter 4:11
471 *Id.*

Practical righteousness in relationship to one another – 12:9-16

12:9 *"Let love be without hypocrisy. Abhor what is evil; cling to what is good.*

12:10 *Be devoted to one another in brotherly love; give preference to one another in honor;*

12:11 *not lagging behind in diligence, fervent in spirit, serving the Lord;*

12:12 *rejoicing in hope, persevering in tribulation, devoted to prayer,*

12:13 *contributing to the needs of the saints, practicing hospitality.*

12:14 *Bless those who persecute you; bless and curse not.*

12:15 *Rejoice with those who rejoice, and weep with those who weep.*

12:16 *Be of the same mind toward one another; do not be haughty in mind, but associate with the lowly. Do not be wise in your own estimation."*

In verses 9 through 16, Paul broadens the discussion from the matter of spiritual gifts and writes of character traits that should characterize all of us. One of the phrases you see repeatedly is "one another." Many years ago, when I was a young Christian, I was challenged to do a study of the phrase "one another" in the New Testament. We are to care for one another;[472] teach one another;[473] admonish one another;[474]

---

472 *See* Ephesians 4:32
473 *See* Colossians 3:16
474 *Id.*

216 • A BRIEF EXPOSITION OF ROMANS

encourage one another;[475] confess our sins to one another,[476] and pray for one another.[477]

Perhaps the phrase that could be considered the great umbrella over the whole paragraph is the very first one – "Let love be without hypocrisy." Jesus said, "By this all men will know that you are My disciples, if you have love for one another."[478] Each time the Bible says what we are to do for one another, you can think of that as a different aspect of loving one another. In one sense, verses 9 through 16 are Paul's description by the Holy Spirit of what loving one another looks like.

- <u>Love is genuine</u>. "Let love be without hypocrisy."[479] We are to love in a genuine way without hypocrisy (play-acting).
- <u>Love is discerning</u>. "Abhor that which is evil; cling to that which is good."[480] This is commonly misunderstood today. Many Christians think that love has no boundaries. The Scripture says that real love is discerning. We abhor what is evil because we know what sin does. "Hate evil, you who love the Lord," the Psalmist says in Psalm 97.[481] We know what sin does to God's children. We must have Spirit-led discernment to fulfill this command in a way that honors God.

---

475 *See* 1 Thessalonians 5:11
476 *See* James 5:16
477 *Id.*
478 John 13:35
479 Romans 12:9
480 *Id.*
481 Psalms 97:10

- Love is Caring. "Contributing to the needs of the saints; given to hospitality."[482] This is generosity — taking care of each other and practicing hospitality. Paul said earlier regarding our gifting, to give with liberality.[483] It brings glory to God when we take care of one another; love one another in practical ways and contribute to the needs of the saints.

- Love is empathetic. "Rejoice with those who rejoice, and weep with those who weep."[484] Many who have been through difficult times have told me how meaningful it has been to have had the presence of other believers weeping with them. Think of Jesus in John Chapter 11 when He came to the scene of his friend Lazarus' death. He did not merely announce, "I have victory over death."[485] He did announce that, and He does have victory over death, and He was going to raise Lazarus from the dead, but first the Bible reads, "Jesus wept."[486] Jesus wept with those who wept. This is empathy.

- Love is praying. In verse 12, we are asked to be "devoted to prayer." One of the most practical things we can do is to pray for one another, to be devoted to prayer. The term devote is used almost exclusively in the New Testament in connection with prayer. In the early church, the apostles devoted themselves to prayer. "We will devote ourselves to prayer and to the ministry of the Word."[487] One of the

---

482 Romans 12:13
483 Romans 12:8
484 Romans 12:15
485 *See e.g.,* Matthew 16:21
486 John 11:35
487 Acts 6:4. *See also* Acts 1:14 and Colossians 4:2

few times this term is not used in relation to prayer gives us understanding as to what it means to be devoted. In the Gospel of Mark, when the crowds were pressing in on Jesus at the edge of the seashore, He stepped back and told His disciples "that a boat should stand ready for Him."[488] Mark uses this same term – the boat was <u>devoted</u> to Him – it was standing ready for His use. If at any time Jesus wanted to step into the boat so that he could preach, it was ready. You and I should be ready at all times to pray.

In the last verse in this section, verse 16, Paul calls us to "be of the same mind toward one another." He again warns about pride. "Do not be haughty in mind … Do not be wise in your own estimation."[489] This is right where he started in verse 3 and is worth repeating. A renewed mind is a humble mind. "God is opposed to the proud, but gives grace to the humble."[490] God is opposed to the proud preacher who strikes his staff and lord's it over his flock.[491] God is opposed to the proud rich man who looks down on others. In all our relationships with one another, we are to be characterized by humility. "Come to Me, all who are weary and heavy-laden, and I will give you rest," Jesus said. "Take My yoke upon you and learn from Me, for I am gentle and humble in heart."[492]

488 Mark 3:9
489 Romans 12:16
490 James 4:6
491 *See* 1 Peter 5:3
492 Matthew 11:28-29

Practical righteousness in relationship to unbelievers – 12:17-21

12:17 *"Never pay back evil for evil to anyone. Respect what is right in the sight of all men.*

12:18 *If possible, so far as it depends on you, be at peace with all men.*

12:19 *Never take your revenge, beloved, but leave room for the wrath of God, for it is written, 'Vengeance is Mine; I will repay, says the Lord.'*

12:20 *'But if your enemy is hungry, feed him, and if he is thirsty, given him a drink; for in so doing you will heap burning coals upon his head.'*

12:21 *Do not be overcome by evil, but overcome evil with good."*

In this last section, Paul moves from instructing about our relationships with one another to teaching about our relationship with those outside the body of Christ. He begins, do not "pay back evil for evil." Do not take your own revenge. As much as it is possible, "be at peace with all men."[493] Jesus said, "Love your enemies and pray for those who persecute you."[494] Do good to those who do evil to you. If they strike you on the cheek, turn the other cheek.[495] Paul expands on this in these verses. Paul is not speaking about the governing authorities at this point. We will see in Romans Chapter 13 that it is the proper role of the government to punish evildoers, but that

---

493 *See* Romans 12:17-19
494 Matthew 5:44
495 *See* Matthew 5:39

220 BRIEF EXPOSITION OF ROMANS

is not our job as individual believers. We are to be peaceable and not take our own revenge.

The final verse is a great summary of all these responsibilities. "Do not be overcome by evil, but overcome evil with good."[496] This kind of living can only be produced by the Holy Spirit. In light of all the mercies of God, Paul said, "Present your bodies [to Him] a living and holy sacrifice."[497] This is pleasing to God. It will not be living like the world; conformed to everybody else's standard. It is a transformed lifestyle, changed from the inside out as we renew our minds and spend time with Him. He changes us from within. We think differently. This transformation will work its way out in our relationships with one another, and God is glorified. We are the body of Christ. Jesus says to us, "You are the light of the world."[498] "Let your light shine ... that they may see your good works, and glorify your Father who is in heaven."[499]

---

496 Romans 12:21
497 Romans 12:1
498 Matthew 5:14
499 Matthew 5:16

Study questions

- What does it mean to be a "living and holy sacrifice" (12:1)?

- How would you describe the importance of being "transformed by the renewing of your mind" (12:2)?

- Why does Paul give the analogy of being "many members in one body" when describing our spiritual gifts? (See 12:3-8).

- How can we show practical righteousness in relationship to "one another"?

- Why, as Christians, are we called not to take our own revenge?

16

PRACTICAL RIGHTEOUSNESS IN RELATIONSHIP TO CIVIL GOVERNMENT

Romans 13

Romans Chapter 13 gives us the Christian view, the right response, to governing authorities. Paul wrote this when the government he was living under was not good. But under the inspiration of the Holy Spirit, he gives us timeless principles for responding to civil government.

How we should respond to civil government – 13:1-7

13:1 *"Let every person be in subjection to the governing authorities. For there is no authority except from God, and those which exist are established by God.*

13:2 *Therefore he who resists authority has opposed the ordinance of God; and they who have opposed will receive condemnation upon themselves.*

13:3 *For rulers are not a cause of fear for good behavior, but for evil. Do you want to have no fear of authority? Do what is good, and you will have praise from the same;* **13:4** *for it is a minister of God to you for good. But if you do what is evil, be afraid; for it does not bear the sword for nothing; for it is a minister of God, an avenger who brings wrath upon the one who practices evil.*
13:5 *Wherefore it is necessary to be in subjection, not only because of wrath, but also for conscience' sake.*
13:6 *For because of this you also pay taxes, for rulers are servants of God, devoting themselves to this very thing.*
13:7 *Render to all what is due them: tax to whom tax is due; custom to whom custom; fear to whom fear; honor to whom honor."*

We will look at this section about the government under three basic headings: its origin, its God-given function, and our responsibility.

The origin of government

God established governments. He instituted it; it was God's idea. The Bible begins with man, Adam and Eve, in perfect harmony. As soon as they sinned and turned away from God, gross sin, immorality, and violence entered the world. Their son, Cain, murdered their other son, Abel. The first few chapters of Genesis spiral downward to where God, in Noah's day, looks around and sees that everything man thinks about is evil.[500] It got so bad that God "was sorry that He had made

---

500 *See Genesis 6:5*

man."[501] For a hundred and twenty years, Noah preached righteousness[502], but no one listened. Finally, God brought judgment on the world. He brought the flood, and He started over with Noah. As soon as Noah and his family got off the ark, God established the principle of human government to control the awful sinfulness of society. "Whoever shed's man's blood, By man his blood should be shed."[503]

Paul writes in verse 1 that the governing authorities which exist are established by God. Our Lord Jesus Himself willingly stood before Pontius Pilate. When we say governments are established by God, we are not saying they are always good. Paul was living under a tyrant, Emperor Nero, at the time he wrote Romans, and there have been many more throughout history. There are varying governments in our world today and they can be far from perfect, but they are nonetheless under God's sovereign authority.

The function of government – 13:3-4

The function of government is pretty simple: The Bible says it is for the praise of those who do right and the punishment of evildoers[504]—in other words, for our protection. "Do what is good, and you will have praise from [the authorities] ... But if you do what is evil, be afraid; for it does not bear the sword for nothing; for it is a minister of God."[505] It is amazing to hear

---

501 Genesis 6:6
502 Genesis 6:3, II Peter 2:5
503 Genesis 9:6
504 I Peter 2:13,14
505 Romans 13:3-4

Paul state that the government is actually a tool of God, "a minister of God." That is what God wants human government to do. This is government's legitimate function: to praise those who do right and punish those who do evil. Governments have not always done that, but that is what God intended.

Our responsibility to government – 13:1-7

Verses 1-7 summarize our responsibility to the government. As Christians, we are to respond to authority with practical righteousness. We have been declared righteous and that should work its way out in our lives in submission to the governing authorities.[506] Do not resist authority.[507] "Our [real] citizenship is in heaven, from which also we eagerly wait for a Savior."[508] We have a dual citizenship. We are citizens of heaven, and we are also citizens of the nation in which we live. We are to submit to the government as unto God. We are to obey it, honor it, and pay taxes.[509]

In Matthew 17, the authorities came to Capernaum and asked Peter, "Does your teacher not pay the two-drachma [temple] tax?"[510] Peter, without really knowing the answer, said, "Yes." He then went to ask Jesus, but before he could speak, Jesus said,

---

506 *See* Romans 13:1
507 *See* Romans 13:2
508 Philippians 3:20
509 *See* Romans 13:7
510 Matthew 17:24

> *"'From whom do the kings of the earth collect customs or poll-tax, from their sons or from strangers?' And upon him saying, 'From strangers,' Jesus said to him, 'Consequently the sons are exempt. But lest we give them offense, go to the sea, and throw in a hook, and take the first fish that comes up; and when you open its mouth, you will find a stater* [a coin in the perfect amount to pay both Jesus' and Peter's tax]. *Take that and give it to them for you and Me.'"*[511]

Our Lord paid the temple tax even though He knew it would not be used properly. We do not pay taxes because we necessarily agree with what is done with it. We pay taxes because human government comes from God.

We are to submit to the government, but this submission is not absolute. The Bible teaches that, "We must obey God rather than men."[512] This is what Peter and the apostles answered when they were commanded by the Sanhedrin Council not to preach in Jesus' name. But this is the exception to the rule. Our responsibility is to submit to the government. The two exceptions are both illustrated for us in the book of Daniel. If the government commands what God forbids, we must obey God rather than man. In Daniel 3, the people were commanded to bow down and worship a golden image. Shadrach, Meshach and Abednego refused do so, and were thrown into the furnace (from which they were delivered by God). The government was demanding what God forbids, and they respectfully disobeyed.

---

511 Matthew 17:25-27
512 Acts 4:18-20, 5:29

The other exception is if the government forbids what God commands. In Daniel 6, a law was passed prohibiting praying for 30 days to anyone other than the King. The government was trying to forbid what God commanded, and Daniel continued to pray to the Lord. Those are the two broad categories of when we would not submit to government, but rather to the higher authority of God.

I would add one more thing that the Bible teaches regarding our responsibility toward government: prayer. Paul wrote Timothy, "I urge that entreaties and prayers, ... be made on behalf of all men, ... and all who are in authority [over you]."[513] Pray for your local and national leaders. God told us to.

Our relationship to the Law – 13:8-10

13:8 *"Owe nothing to anyone except to love one another; for he who loves his neighbor has fulfilled the law.*
13:9 *For this, 'You shall not commit adultery, you shall not murder, You shall not steal, You shall not covet,' and if there is any other commandment, it is summed up in this saying, 'You should love your neighbor as yourself.'*
13:10 *Love does no wrong to a neighbor; love therefore is the fulfillment of the law.*

In verses 8-10, Paul summarizes practical righteousness in relationship to God's laws — the commandments. We have seen in Romans that God's law cannot justify or sanctify us. But He still wants for us what the law required: holy living.

---
513   1 Timothy 2:1-2

In Romans 8, we saw that the Holy Spirit enables us to live holy lives and fulfill the requirement of the Law.[514] Paul here says you can sum this all up in love. He who loves his neighbor has fulfilled the law toward his neighbor.[515] All the other commandments can be summed up, he says, by this one — to "love your neighbor as yourself."[516] Love will not steal, will not covet, will not commit adultery. God is a God of love. "By this all men will know that you are my disciples, if you have love for one another."[517] Love is the fulfillment of the law toward one another, and we know from our Lord's words that love is the fulfillment of the commandments toward God. We are to love the Lord with everything we have and love our neighbor as our self.[518] "We love because He first loved us."[519]

The Christian and the return of Christ – 13:11-14

13:11 *"And this do, knowing the time, that it is already the hour for you to awaken from sleep; for now salvation is nearer to us than when we believed.*

13:12 *The night is almost gone, and the day is at hand. Let us therefore lay aside the deeds of darkness and put on the armor of light.*

---

514   *See* Romans 8:4
515   *See* Romans 13:10
516   Romans 13:9
517   John 13:35
518   *See* Matthew 22:36-39
519   1 John 4:19

> **13:13** *Let us behave properly as in the day, not in carousing and drunkenness, not in sexual promiscuity and sensuality, not in strife and jealousy.*
> **13:14** *But put on the Lord Jesus Christ, and make no provision for the flesh in regard to its lusts."*

It is time for us to "awaken from sleep, for our salvation is nearer to us than when we believed." I mentioned the tenses of salvation earlier.[520] God's gospel brings a full salvation; a full deliverance. In the past we were delivered from the penalty of our sin – justification. As we grow, we are being delivered from the power of sin – sanctification. And one day soon, when Jesus returns, we will be delivered from the very presence of sin – glorification. Our salvation is nearer to us than it was yesterday.[521]

Augustine (Augustine of Hippo) was an important early church leader. But he was anything but a saint in his early life. He lived a hedonistic lifestyle, engaging in drunkenness, sexual promiscuity, and other immoral behavior. His life was about self. But he was left empty inside. Sin never satisfies. He picked up the book of Romans and read this text, Romans 13:11-14, and it brought him to Jesus Christ. We know him as St. Augustine, a great theologian who wrote so much that has helped guide us as believers through the centuries. He was changed from the inside out like any sinner is who comes to Jesus Christ and puts their faith in Him.

---

520 *See* discussion of Romans 8:28-30, session 12, *supra*.
521 *See* Romans 13:11

Augustine learned what you and I need to learn. Living for self, living for pleasure, living for what this world has to offer, leaves you empty. It leaves you in despair. You might put on a good front, even living for good things like family, or just to be a nice person, but if your bottom line is just what you want, what you can do on your own, it leaves you longing for something more. Chapter 13 ends, like Romans passages often do, by bringing us back to home base. "Put on the Lord Jesus Christ."[522] Augustine was not saved by Christianity. He was not transformed by turning over a new leaf. He was saved by a person, Jesus Christ, and was changed from the inside out.

The fact that Jesus is returning governs the Christian life. We eagerly await His return. As you read through the New Testament, you will see that the return of Jesus is linked to practical righteous living. Be alert in praying.[523] Be on the watch and live a pure life because your master is coming back.[524] He "who has his hope fixed on Him purifies himself, just as He is pure."[525] James 5 says, to be patient like the farmer because He is coming back.[526] Wait for the early and late rains, because "the Judge is standing right at the door."[527] Hebrews 10, refers to Jesus' return by saying, "For yet in a very little while, He who is coming will come, and will not delay."[528] We long for the return of Jesus.

---

522 Romans 13:14
523 *See* 1 Peter 4:7
524 *See* Matthew 24:42
525 1 John 3:3
526 *See* James 5:7
527 James 5:9
528 Hebrews 10:37

Study questions

- What are the origin and functions of government?

- According to scripture, what is our responsibility to civil government? How did Christ exemplify this?

- How should the fact that Jesus is returning ("for now salvation is nearer to us than when we believed," 13:11) shape the Christian life?

17

RIGHTEOUS LIVING IN RELATIONSHIP TO WEAKER BRETHREN
Romans 14:1–15:3

Chapter 13 instructs us regarding our relationship to human government. Now Chapter 14 speaks of righteous living in relationship to weaker brethren. The weaker brother or sister is not necessarily shaky in their faith but rather over-scrupulous about things that are really only matters of conscience. We will see that sometimes the weaker brother or sister has a long list of things they do or do not do to seek to be devoted to Christ, and this chapter gives us instruction as to how we should respond to that person. I will say at the outset what Paul says in verse 1, we are to accept them. He says later that we are to walk "according to love."[529]

If we learn to follow what Paul is teaching in Chapter 14, it will bring much glory to God because it will lead to unity among the brethren and will spare us much discord in the church. God is always glorified when brothers and sisters live together in unity.

---

529 Romans 14:15

I have been referring to Chapter 14, but how we respond to weaker brothers and sisters will not conclude until 15:17. "With one accord you may with one voice glorify the God and Father of our Lord Jesus Christ."[530] In other words, Paul wants us to be of the same mind, bringing weaker and stronger brothers and sisters together to glorify God with unity.

Romans Chapters 12 through 16 are all about life and living. Some matters in life are clearly right or wrong; "you shall not," "you shall." We saw the commandments, for example, in Chapter 13 where God says, "You shall not steal, You shall not covet; ... You shall love your neighbor as yourself."[531] But many other things are left to our conscience. Paul here refers to dietary restrictions and observance of days, so I will as well, but we can expand this to many other things that are matters of style or preference. Sometimes Christians are tempted to divide over style, such as different types of music. God did not tell us anything about this in the sense of one style or the other being right or wrong. We have a tendency to go beyond what God says and expect our brothers and sisters to live according to our personal standards in matters which He left open for us to have personal discretion and liberty.

The chapter can be outlined in two sections: the first half, verses 1-12, is our Christian liberty: accept without judging. The second half, verses 13 to the end, deal with limitations on that liberty: live without hindering. Do not cause your brother to stumble.

---

530 Romans 15:6
531 Romans 13:9

Our Christian liberty – 14:1-12

14:1 *"Now accept the one who is weak in faith, but not for the purpose of passing judgment on his opinions.*

14:2 *One man has faith that he may eat all things, but he who is weak eats vegetables only.*

14:3 *Let not him who eats regard with contempt him who does not eat, and let not him who does not eat judge him who eats, for God has accepted him.*

14:4 *Who are you to judge the servant of another? To his own master he stands or falls; and stand he will, for the Lord is able to make him stand.*

14:5 *One man regards one day above another, another regards every day alike. Let each man be fully convinced in his own mind.*

14:6 *He who observes the day, observes it for the Lord, and he who eats, does so for the Lord, for he gives thanks to God; and he who eats not, for the Lord he does not eat, and gives thanks to God."*

Verse 1 begins, "Now accept the one who is weak in faith, but not for the purpose of passing judgment on his opinions." Accept him because God has.[532] Somewhat surprisingly, Paul describes the one who is a religious vegetarian, who says, "I will not eat meat, I will only eat vegetables in order to be more devout as a Christian," as the weaker brother.[533] Christians who make long lists of prohibitions about things the Bible is silent on are the weaker ones. The pathway to strength and devotion to Christ is not a lot of extra things we have to do or

---

532 *See* Romans 14:3
533 *See* Romans 14:2

236 · A BRIEF EXPOSITION OF ROMANS

not do. If you have been a Christian for any length of time, you
have probably observed this behavior. There is a tendency for
some to come up with prohibitions that they think will make
us stronger for the Lord. Paul says that is the weaker brother
or sister. But we are to accept them; God has.

Church history is littered with individuals and whole groups
of people who came up with prohibitions or requirements not
found in the Bible. In Paul's day, there was a Jewish tendency
to add circumcision and law-keeping. There was a tendency
among Gentiles to include paganism, eastern mysticism, or
asceticism (severe self-denial), which was practiced in the
Roman Empire. All these approaches were coloring Christians'
thinking and, in more extreme cases, led to outright apostasy.
This kind of thinking can lead to people losing sight of the
cross of Jesus Christ and thinking that Christianity is simply
a bunch of rules and regulations. False teachers often focus
on these sorts of things.

Paul addresses the Jewish thinking in Galatians, saying, "I
fear for you." "You observe days and months and seasons
and years."[534] It got to the point that believers had added
circumcision and law-keeping to the cross. In Colossians, Paul
addresses the pagan asceticism aspect of this, warning,

> *"[Let no one] act as your judge in regard to food or
> drink or in respect to a festival or a new moon or
> a Sabbath day – things which are a mere shadow
> of what is to come; but the substance belongs to*

534 Galatians 4:11 and 10

Christ. Let no one keep defrauding you of your prize by delighting in self-abasement ... If you have died with Christ ... why, as if you were living in the world, do you submit yourself to decrees, such as, 'Do not handle, do not taste, do not touch!'"[535]

In Romans 14, however, Paul is not talking about where these behaviors can actually lead to outright denial of the gospel. He is simply saying that among Christians, there is a liberty to have matters of conscience to do or not do things if the Bible has not spelled it out. We are to accept one another. Romans Chapter 15:1 is a good summary verse: "Now we who are strong ought to bear the weaknesses of those without strength and not just please ourselves."

There are two temptations in this matter of conscience, and they are both given to us in verse 3, "Let not him who eats regard with contempt him who does not eat, and let not him who does not eat judge him who eats, for God has accepted him." Do not glory in your liberty saying, I am free to eat and drink, and then regard with contempt those who do not believe that they have that freedom. On the other hand, do not glory in your abstinence and your observances of days, and judge others who do not follow your standard. Those who demonstrate the attitudes described in verse 3 are not "walking according to love"[536] and are not filled with the Holy Spirit but often filled with pride.

---

535 Colossians 2:16-18; 20-21
536 Romans 14:15

The overriding principle is stated in verse 4, "Who are you to judge the servant of another? To his own master he stands or falls; and stand he will, for the Lord is able to make him stand."[537] You are not your brother's lord and master. Do not meddle; do not impose your standards on others. Do not judge them. Do not regard your brother and sister with contempt. "One man regards one day above another, another regards every day alike. Let each man be fully convinced in his own mind."[538] That is why I say dietary restrictions, observance of days and the like are left to one's conscience. One person feels you should never do a particular thing on the Lord's Day, another person regards every day the same and says, "if you shouldn't do it on the Lord's Day, then you shouldn't do it on Monday, Tuesday, or Wednesday." Paul just says, "Let each man be fully convinced in his own mind.[539]

Give account to God – 14:7-12

14:7 *"For not one of us lives for himself, and not one dies for himself;*

14:8 *for if we live, we live for the Lord, or if we die, we die for the Lord; therefore whether we live or die, we are the Lord's.*

14:9 *For to this end Christ died and lived again, that He might be Lord both of the dead and of the living.*

---

537   Romans 14:4
538   Romans 14:5
539   Romans 14:5

14:10 *But you, why do you judge your brother? Or you again, why do you regard your brother with contempt? For we will also stand before the judgment seat of God.* **14:11** *For it is written, 'As I live, says the Lord, every knee will bow to Me. And every tongue will give praise to God.'* **14:12** *So then each one of us will give account of himself to God."*

Paul continues to teach us in verses 7-12. Jesus Christ is the Lord. Jesus Christ is the judge. We will all give account to Him.[540] Five times in this paragraph, he says, do all that you do for the Lord. In these matters, give thanks to God. Twice he says, if we live, we live for the Lord. If we die, we die for the Lord. We have amazing Christian liberty in matters that are not ultimately right or wrong because they have not been spelled out in Scripture.

Limitation on our Liberty – 14:13-23; 15:1-3

If we just stop at these verses, we might think the Christian life was to be lived just between the Lord and us. This could lead to a kind of isolationism or individualism. But we have been born into God's family. One of the things that I tell a brother who has just received Jesus Christ is, "Welcome to the family, brother." We are to live in community. "We, who are many, are one body in Christ, and individually members one of another."[541] Accordingly, the last half of Romans Chapter 14 presents limitations on our liberty. Paul says, accept your

---

540 Romans 14:12
541 Romans 12:5

240 • A BRIEF EXPOSITION OF ROMANS

weaker brother. Do not judge him. He also says, do not cause your brother to stumble.[542]

> **14:13** *"Therefore let us not judge one another anymore, but rather determine this — not to put an obstacle or a stumbling block in a brother's way.*
>
> **14:14** *I know and am convinced in the Lord Jesus that nothing is unclean in itself; but to him who thinks anything to be unclean, to him it is unclean.*
>
> **14:15** *For if because of food your brother is hurt, you are no longer walking according to love. Do not destroy with your food him for whom Christ died.*
>
> **14:16** *Therefore do not let what is for you a good thing be spoken of as evil;*
>
> **14:17** *for the kingdom of God is not eating and drinking, but righteousness and peace and joy in the Holy Spirit.*
>
> **14:18** *For he who in this way serves Christ is acceptable to God and approved by men.*
>
> **14:19** *So then let us pursue the things which make for peace and the building up of one another.*
>
> **14:20** *Do not tear down the work of God for the sake of food. All things indeed are clean, but they are evil for the man who eats and gives offense.*
>
> **14:21** *It is good not to eat meat or to drink wine, or to do anything by which your brother stumbles."*

There is a higher law than liberty, the law of love. We have amazing liberty. Paul had the freedom to eat and not worry about how the meat had been prepared. But there is a higher

---

542 *See* Romans 14:21

principle than just exercising our liberty. "To him who thinks anything to be unclean, to him it is unclean. For if because of food your brother is hurt, you are no longer walking according to love. Do not destroy with your food him for whom Christ died."[543] Christ died for your brother. Do not cause him to stumble or go against his conscience because you have the liberty that he has not learned yet. Surely you can deny yourself some liberties for your brother for whom Christ died.

There are some Christians who spend a lot of energy trying to determine what is permissible in eating and drinking and those kinds of things. Beware of wasting time and energy on such things. The kingdom of God is not what you eat or drink. There are Christians who end up flaunting their liberties, always explaining why they are free to do this or do that. Others spend time watching for those who do things they do not think they should. Many of us who know the Lord have a tendency to be one or the other of these. Paul says, limit your liberty; remember what the kingdom of God is all about, "not eating or drinking, but righteousness and peace and joy in the Holy Spirit."[544] "He who in this way serves Christ is acceptable to God and approved by men."[545] We should not pursue our liberties in grey areas but pursue that which makes "for peace and the building up of one another."[546] He uses that important phrase again, build up "one another."

---

543 Romans 14:14-15
544 Romans 14:17
545 Romans 14:18
546 Romans 14:19

Paul gives a strong warning in verse 20, "Do not tear down the work of God for the sake of food." Do not destroy the work of God flaunting your liberties. "All things indeed are clean, but they are evil for the man who eats and gives offence."[547] Even though someone has liberty, he may give offense to his brother. Paul was happy to limit his own liberty for the sake of the body of Christ. "It is good not to eat meat or to drink wine, or to do anything by which your brother stumbles."[548]

Paul made the same point in a parallel passage in 1 Corinthians regarding the eating of food that had been sacrificed to idols, an issue in the first century. He first notes that "we know that there is no such thing as an idol in the world, and that there is no God but one."[549] Paul goes on to acknowledge, however, that "not all men have this knowledge."[550]

> "Some ... eat food as if it were sacrificed to an idol; and their conscience being weak is defiled. But food will not commend us to God; we are neither the worse if we do not eat, nor the better if we do eat. But take care that this liberty of yours does not somehow become a stumbling block to the weak."[551]

Paul was teaching the same principle, yes, we have liberty, but there are limitations on that liberty. Paul was happy to

---

547   Romans 14:20
548   Romans 14:21
549   1 Corinthians 8:4
550   1 Corinthians 8:7
551   1 Corinthians 8:7-9

limit his own liberty and not eat certain foods if it caused his brother to stumble.

> **14:22** *"The faith which you have, have as your own conviction before God. Happy is he who does not condemn himself in what he approves.*
>
> **14:23** *But he who doubts is condemned if he eats, because his eating is not from faith; and whatever is not from faith is sin.*
>
> **15:1** *Now we who are strong ought to bear the weaknesses of those without strength and not just please ourselves.*
>
> **15:2** *Let each of us please his neighbor for his good, to his edification.*
>
> **15:3** *For even Christ did not please Himself; but as it is written, 'The reproaches of those who reproached You fell upon Me."*

As we look back on these verses, I am reminded of our pre-eminent example, "For even Christ did not please Himself."[552] He sought above all else to please the Father. Jesus said, "For I always do the things that are pleasing to Him."[553] This will lead to a lifestyle like His, which was sacrificial and giving. That is how we are supposed to be; not just to please ourselves. So even though we may have amazing Christian liberty in all these things that the Bible has not specifically called out as right or wrong, we are not merely to please ourselves. Christ died for our brother, so accept the one who is weaker in faith.

---

552 Romans 15:3
553 John 8:29

Do not judge or disdain. Do not cause your brother to stumble. In other words, do not merely please yourself.

Keep in mind the principle that we have been emphasizing throughout this section, "the kingdom of God is not eating or drinking, but righteousness and peace and joy in the Holy Spirit."[554] When you come into church to worship, and the music is not your preferred style, remember that the kingdom of God is not about types of music, eating, and drinking, or any of these secondary things. Do not pursue these things; pursue Christ together in community. "Pursue the things which make for peace and the building up of one another."[555] Pursue our Lord Jesus Christ, who died on our behalf and rose again for our justification.

Study questions

- What does Paul mean when he writes, "accept the one who is weak in faith?"

- What are some practical ways not to cause our brothers and sisters in Christ to stumble?

- What are some examples of issues today causing disunity among Christians over matters Paul would deem unimportant?

---

554 Romans 14:17
555 Romans 14:19

18

CONCLUSION

Romans 15:4–16:27

As we come to the last two chapters of Romans, it is good to look back and briefly summarize. Paul has explained the gospel for 11 chapters; what God has done for us. At the end of his argument, verse 36 of Chapter 11, Paul declares, "For from Him and through Him and to Him are all things. To Him be the glory forever. Amen."[556] It is all about Him, what He did for us.

But this has implications. So, for the balance of Romans, Paul is saying, because of what God has done, "I urge you therefore, brethren, by the mercies of God, to present your bodies a living and holy sacrifice."[557] Paul systematically tells you this is your relationship to God. It should be one of putting yourself on the altar, abandoning yourself to Him. He will not let you down. He loves you. The demonstration of that love is that He sent His Son to die for you when you were helpless and hopeless. When you were nothing but an ungodly enemy of His, He died for you.[558] Paul then writes about our relationship

---

556 Romans 11:36
557 Romans 12:1
558 *See* Romans 5:6-8

246 · A BRIEF EXPOSITION OF ROMANS

to one another (the rest of Chapter 12); our enemies; the civil government (Chapter 13); how we should live in relationship to the return of Jesus Christ (He is coming back!); and then our response to weaker brothers (Chapter 14 to the beginning of Chapter 15). We now look at the remainder of Chapter 15 through the end of Chapter 16 – the conclusion of Romans.

Perseverance and encouragement — 15:4-6

15:4 *"For whatever was written in earlier times was writ-ten for our instruction, that through perseverance and the encouragement of the Scriptures we might have hope.*
15:5 *Now may the God who gives perseverance and encouragement grant you to be of the same mind with one another according to Christ Jesus;*
15:6 *that with one accord you may with one voice glorify the God and Father of our Lord Jesus Christ."*

We all need both perseverance and encouragement. God alone is the source of both.[559] Perseverance is a compound word that has the idea of hanging in there, abiding under, not fleeing from your circumstances. It means when the going gets tough, not saying, "Well, I will just start over." It is not saying, "I'll just find another church" or similar things that we are so prone to—particularly in our culture of lack of commitment. God gives us strength — perseverance, which we all need. He also gives encouragement. He is the Encourager; the *Parakletos*. The word has the same root as helper and comforter. He comes alongside us, and He encourages us. We all desperately need

559 Romans 15:5

encouragement, and God gives it. His Holy Spirit is called the Encourager. You and I need to encourage one another and allow His fruit to be displayed in our daily lives.

How does God give perseverance and encouragement? Look back at verse 4, "Whatever was written in earlier times was written for our instruction, that through perseverance and the encouragement of the Scriptures we might have hope."[560] Do you need perseverance and encouragement? Go to the *"Graphe,"* the Scripture; the written Word of God. The Holy Spirit delights in taking up His Word. He gives us encouragement and perseverance to hang in there. He does it through the Scripture. As we spend time with Him in His written Word, we will find that "whatever was written was written for our instruction."[561]

Verses 5 and 6 are woven together. He desires to bring unity that glorifies Himself. When we spend time in His Word, we are spending time with Him, and He feeds us so that we might be of the same mindset; "that with one accord [we] may with one voice glorify the God and Father of our Lord Jesus Christ."[562] Pray for this for your marriage, that with one voice and one accord, you might glorify God. Pray that for your church. Church unity glorifies God. When we can come around the Person and work of Jesus Christ in unity, with one voice proclaiming Him, it glorifies God.

---

560 Romans 15:4

561 *Id.*

562 Romans 15:6

Rejoice O Gentiles – 15:7-13

15:7 *"Wherefore, accept one another, just as Christ also accepted us to the glory of God.*

15:8 *For I say that Christ has become a servant to the circumcision on behalf of the truth of God to confirm the promises given to the fathers,*

15:9 *and for the Gentiles to glorify God for His mercy; as it is written, 'Therefore I will give praise to You among the Gentiles, and I will sing to Your name.'*

15:10 *And again he says, 'Rejoice, O Gentiles, with His people.'*

15:11 *And again, 'Praise the Lord all you Gentiles, and let all the peoples praise Him.*

15:12 *And again Isaiah says, 'There will come the root of Jesse, and He who arises to rule over the Gentiles, in Him shall the Gentiles hope.'*

15:13 *Now may the God of hope fill you with all joy and peace in believing, that you may abound in hope by the power of the Holy Spirit."*

Paul reinforces what he had said previously that the gospel is "to bring about the obedience of faith among all [the nations]."[563] This is a theme of Romans from the beginning of the Epistle (1:15) to the end (16:26). Paul makes the same point again and again; "For I am not ashamed of the gospel, for it is the power of God for salvation to everyone who believes, to the Jew first and also to the Greek. [Gentile]."[564] Paul says concerning the Jews, "Christ has become a servant

---

563 Romans 1:5 (some translations, *"among all the Gentiles"*)
564 Romans 1:16

to the circumcision on behalf of the truth of God to confirm the promises given to the fathers."[565] Christ saves Jews; He is the servant to the circumcision. He confirms His promises. He is glorified in being faithful. He is not done with Israel. As Paul explains in Romans Chapter 11, although there has been "a partial hardening"[566] of Israel, in God's timing, He will bring Israel back into a state of belief. "All Israel will be saved; just as it is written, 'The Deliverer will come from Zion, He will remove ungodliness from Jacob.'"[567] God saves Jew and Gentile alike, but when He saves Jews, it is particularly to emphasize His faithfulness to His promises.

God also saves Gentiles "to glorify God for His mercy."[568] Paul quotes several passages emphasizing that the Old Testament predicted the Messiah would deliver all nations (Gentiles).[569] In verse 11, he quotes Psalms 117, the shortest Psalm in the Bible, with the burst of praise, "Praise the Lord all you Gentiles, and let all the peoples praise Him."[570] Paul is habitually quoting the Scriptures because the gospel flows from the Old Testament.

Verse 13 gives the great benediction, "Now may the God of hope fill you with all joy and peace in believing, that you may abound in hope by the power of the Holy Spirit." In times of darkness and despair, remember that God is the God of hope. Turn to Him through His Word and find hope; just like Paul said

---

565 Romans 15:8
566 Romans 11:25
567 Romans 11:26
568 Romans 15:9
569 Psalms 18:49-50 and 117:1; Deuteronomy 32:43; and Isaiah 11:10
570 Romans 15:11

in verse 4, "that through perseverance and the encouragement of the Scriptures we might have hope."

Paul's missionary heart — 15:14-21

15:14 *"And concerning you, my brethren, I myself also am convinced that you yourselves are full of goodness, filled with all knowledge, and able also to admonish one another.*

15:15 *But I have written very boldly to you on some points, so as to remind you again, because of the grace that was given me from God,*

15:16 *to be a minister of Christ Jesus to the Gentiles, ministering as a priest the gospel of God, that my offering of the Gentiles might become acceptable, sanctified by the Holy Spirit.*

15:17 *Therefore in Christ Jesus I have found reason for boasting in things pertaining to God.*

15:18 *For I will not presume to speak of anything except what Christ has accomplished through me, resulting in the obedience of the Gentiles by word and deed,*

15:19 *in the power of signs and wonders, in the power of the Spirit; so that from Jerusalem and round about as far as Illyricum I have fully preached the gospel of Christ.*

15:20 *And thus I aspired to preach the gospel, not where Christ was already named, that I might not build upon another man's foundation:*

15:21 *but as it is written, 'They who had no news of Him will see, and they who have not heard will understand.'"*

In these verses, we see Paul's joyous heart for the healthy congregation at Rome. Paul had a shepherd's heart, but he mentions his missionary heart as well. Every pastor should have both a shepherd's heart and a missionary's heart. He tells us, I will not speak of what I have done, but what God has done through me in bringing about the obedience of faith among the Gentiles by word and deed.[571] The gospel brings about a life transformation, and Paul's ministry among the Gentiles has resulted in just that — obedience by word and deed. We also see Paul's pioneering heart; "I aspired to preach the gospel, not where Christ was already named, that I might not build upon another man's foundation."[572] God had put it on his heart to go where the gospel had not yet been heard. God is still at work creating pioneer hearts in His people. It is exciting when as a church, we can be a part of, and involved with, missionaries who take the gospel out into the far reaches.

Christian giving – 15:22-29

15:22 *"For this reason I have often been hindered from coming to you;*

15:23 *but now, with no further place for me in these regions, and since I have had for many years a longing to come to you*

15:24 *whenever I go to Spain – for I hope to see you in passing, and to be helped on my way there by you, when I have first enjoyed your company for awhile –*

15:25 *but now, I am going to Jerusalem serving the saints.*

---

571   Romans 15:18
572   Romans 15:20

15:26 *For Macedonia and Achaia have been pleased to make a contribution for the poor among the saints in Jerusalem.*

15:27 *Yes, they were pleased to do so, and they are indebted to them. For if the Gentiles have shared in their spiritual things, they are indebted to minister to them also in material things.*

15:28 *Therefore, when I have finished this, and have put my seal on this fruit of theirs, I will go on by way of you to Spain.*

15:29 *And I know that when I come to you, I will come in the fullness of the blessing of Christ."*

Paul had never been to Rome. He was eager to go and see and encourage the believers who were there. He begins In Chapter 1 saying, "I do not want you to be unaware, brethren, that often I have planned to come to you (and have been prevented thus far)."[573] But he wanted to get there, and now he reiterates, "I have had for many years a longing to come to you."[574] Although he was headed back to Jerusalem to the East, he was already planning and praying to go to the furthest, western-most region of the then known world: Spain. And he hoped "to be helped on my way there by"[575] the brethren in Rome. That is always necessary as we send the gospel out; it takes money. We are all to be involved in this great mission. Someone has said there are three kinds of Christians: those who go, those

---

573 Romans 1:13
574 Romans 15:23
575 Romans 15:24

who send them, and those who are disobedient. We must all be involved in getting God's Word out.

Paul mentions another type of Christian giving. Why is he going to Jerusalem? Because despite their own poverty, the church in Macedonia and Achaia were "pleased to make a contribution for the poor among the saints in Jerusalem,"[576] and Paul felt that it was so important, he was personally going to deliver it. Paul writes of their giving in 2 Corinthians,

> "Now, brethren, we wish to make known to you the grace of God which has been given in the churches of Macedonia, that in a great ordeal of affliction their abundance of joy and their deep poverty overflowed in the wealth of their liberality. For I testify that according to their ability, and beyond their ability, they gave of their own accord."[577]

When they did not have anything, they gave. They gave out of joy. "God loves a cheerful giver."[578] The Macedonian church gave joyously and cheerfully out of deep poverty because they knew of the need in Jerusalem. This was a picture of the Jewish-Gentile unity. Paul is saying, if they benefited from the Jerusalem church in spiritual things, they are indebted to them "to minister to them also in material things."[579] Giving is part of the very fabric of knowing Christ. We serve and love a

---

576 Romans 15:26
577 2 Corinthians 8:1-3
578 2 Corinthians 9:7
579 Romans 15:27

254 · A BRIEF EXPOSITION OF ROMANS

God who gave. When He comes into our lives, it is part of our nature to want to give.

Strive in Prayer – 15:30-33

15:30 *"Now I urge you, brethren, by our Lord Jesus Christ and by the love of the Spirit, to strive together with me in your prayers to God for me,*

15:31 *that I may be delivered from those who are disobedient in Judea, and that my service for Jerusalem may prove acceptable to the saints;*

15:32 *so that I may come to you in joy by the will of God and find refreshing rest in your company.*

15:33 *Now the God of peace be with you all. Amen."*

Paul urges his brethren to "strive together [to *"synagonizomai"* — to exert one's strength – we get our word to agonize from the root of this verb] with me in your prayers to God for me."[580] Agonize in prayer; prayer is hard work. Paul uses the related term, *"agonizomai,"* when he says, "Fight the good fight."[581] Struggle! Wrestle! Do you find prayer hard? Agonize with Paul, who found it hard. Luke describes our Lord Jesus Christ in Gethsemane: "And being in an agony He was praying very fervently; and His sweat became like drops of blood."[582] When we struggle in prayer, we are involved in the very activity that our Lord agonized in. Paul has told us that even when we do not know how to pray as we should, the Holy Spirit

---

580 Romans 15:30
581 1 Timothy 6:12
582 Luke 22:44

intercedes for us.[583] God the Son and God the Spirit are praying; you and I should be too.

Our struggle is not against flesh and blood; it is a spiritual battle.[584] We will never know, this side of eternity, how much of the battle was won by people quietly praying. Prayer does not always turn out the way we want. Paul said, pray that I would be able to get to Judea and get to Rome and then be on my way to Spain. Paul got to Rome, but it was in chains. It did not turn out the way he had planned, but God works His purposes through those who pray, even though we do not always understand the full mystery.

Greetings to those at Rome – 16:1-16

16:1 *"I commend to you our sister Phoebe, who is a servant of the church which is at Cenchrea;*

16:2 *that you receive her in the Lord in a manner worthy of the saints, and that you help her in whatever matter she may have need of you; for she herself has also been a helper of many, and of myself as well.*

16:3 *Greet Prisca and Aquila my fellow-workers in Christ Jesus,*

16:4 *who for my life risked their own necks, to whom not only do I give thanks, but also all the churches of the Gentiles;*

---

583   *See* Romans 8:26
584   *See* Ephesians 6:12

> **16:5** *also greet the church that is in their house. Greet Epaenetus my beloved, who is the first convert to Christ from Asia."*

In this final chapter, Paul sends greetings to many people in Rome. He greets his "fellow workers in Christ," Prisca and Aquila, who had risked their own lives for Paul's sake. There is nothing like the camaraderie of fellow workers in Christ. Prisca and Aquila had to flee Italy when Claudius Caesar commanded all the Jews to leave Rome. They landed in Corinth, where Paul met them. They were "of the same trade" (tentmakers). He stayed with them, and they labored in the gospel together, and later he took them with him to Ephesus.[585]

Paul then greets "Epaenetus my beloved, who is the first convert to Christ from Asia."[586] Missionaries always remember their first convert. Dr. Rick Calenberg, the former International Director of the Romans Project, shares about the first person he led to Christ when he arrived in Nigeria – Dan Luke. Rick remembers him as a 15-year-old kid hungry to follow the Lord. He took him with him wherever he went. More than twenty-five years later, Dan is ministering to hundreds of university students, and there has been great, ongoing fruitfulness of life.

> **16:6** *Greet Mary, who has worked hard for you.*
> **16:7** *Greet Andronicus and Junias, my kinsmen, and my fellow-prisoners, who are outstanding among the apostles, who also were in Christ before me.*

---

585 *See* Acts 18:1-3; 18-19
586 Romans 16:5

16:8 *Greet Ampliatus my beloved in the Lord.*

16:9 *Greet Urbanus our fellow-worker in Christ, and Stachys my beloved.*

16:10 *Greet Apelles, the approved in Christ. Greet those who are of the household of Aristobulus.*

16:11 *Greet Herodion my kinsman. Greet those of the household of Narcissus, who are in the Lord.*

16:12 *Greet Tryphaena and Tryphosa, workers in the Lord. Greet Persis the beloved, who has worked hard in the Lord.*

16:13 *Greet Rufus, a choice man in the Lord, also his mother and mine.*

16:14 *Greet Asyncritus, Phlegon, Hermes, Patrobas, Hermas and the brethren with them.*

16:15 *Greet Philologus and Julia, Nereus and his sister, and Olympas, and all the saints who are with them.*

16:16 *Greet one another with a holy kiss. All the churches of Christ greet you."*

We may not know who all these people were, but they are written down in God's Word. The Scripture tells us He knows us by name. Imagine if your name was written in the book – the Bible. If you believe in Jesus Christ, your name is written in The Book – the book of life. "He who overcomes will thus be clothed in white garments; and I will not erase his name from the book of life, and I will confess his name before My Father."[587]

There is a story behind each name; we may not know it, but there is a story. In verse 13, he writes, "Greet Rufus, a choice

587 Revelation 3:5

man in the Lord, also his mother and mine." Rufus' mother was like a mother to him, as if they had possibly taken Paul into their home. In the Gospel of Mark's account of when Simon was commandeered, "That he might bear [Jesus'] cross," Mark notes that he was "the father of Alexander and Rufus."[588] It is exciting to see the human element and inter-connectedness of these accounts.

Twice Paul mentions how those he greets had "worked hard" in the Lord. The word suggests working hard until exhaustion. Do not be discouraged when you are working hard for the Lord if you become tired. Paul uses the same term writing to Timothy, "The hard-working farmer ought to be first to receive his share of the crops."[589] God honors hard work.

Watch out for false teachings — 16:17-20

16:17 *"Now I urge you, brethren, keep your eye on those who cause dissensions and hindrances contrary to the teaching which you learned, and turn away from them.*
16:18 *For such men are slaves not of our Lord Christ but of their own appetites; and by their smooth and flattering speech they deceive the hearts of the unsuspecting.*
16:19 *For the report of your obedience has reached to all; therefore I am rejoicing over you, but I want you to be wise in what is good, and innocent in what is evil.*
16:20 *And the God of peace will soon crush Satan under your feet."*

588 Mark 15:21
589 2 Timothy 2:6

Up to this point, Paul has not had to give warnings to the church in Rome. He was not dealing with specific issues, as he had to in other epistles. Nonetheless, he issues a final warning at the conclusion of his letter, saying, watch out for false teaching. False teachers (false brethren) cause dissensions.[590] "Reject a factious man after a first and second warning."[591] There is something wrong when someone is eager to create dissension and factiousness. You can know that such a person has a bad heart. "For such men are slaves not of our Lord Christ but of their own appetites."[592] False teachers are often in it for their own appetites (literally, their own belly). Without Christ, we live for food, pleasure, money, power, pride, and what people think of us. And false teachers can be smooth. "By their smooth and flattering speech they deceive the hearts of the unsuspecting."[593]

He concludes this section by saying, "And the God of peace will soon crush Satan under your feet."[594] God dealt with Satan at the cross, but he is still prowling around like a roaring lion.[595] He will soon be crushed under the feet of the Lord's church. There is coming a day—we read about it in the Book of Revelation, the last book of the Bible—when Satan is thrown into the lake of fire, no longer to harass and deceive the nations.[596] We long for that day.

---

590 Romans 16:17
591 Titus 3:10
592 Romans 16:18
593 *Id.*
594 Romans 16:20
595 *See* 1 Peter 5:8
596 *See* Revelation 20:10

Final greetings and Doxology — 16:21-27

16:21 *"Timothy my fellow-worker greets you; and so do Lucius and Jason and Sosipater,   my kinsmen.*

16:22 *I Tertius, who write this letter,*[597] *greet you in the Lord.*

16:23 *Gaius, host to me and to the whole church, greets you. Erastus, the city treasurer greets you, and Quartus, the brother.*

16:24 [The grace of our Lord Jesus Christ be with you all. Amen.]

16:25 *Now to Him who is able to establish you according to my gospel and the preaching of Jesus Christ, according to the revelation of the mystery which has been kept secret for long ages past,*

16:26 *but now is manifested, and by the Scriptures of the prophets, according to the commandment of the eternal God, has been made known to all the nations, leading to obedience of faith;*

16:27 *to the only wise God, through Jesus Christ, be the glory forever. Amen."*

Paul started with the gospel of God, and he closes with it. I quoted John Mitchell earlier who told me, "If you get well established in Romans, you are well established." Paul said back in Chapter 1, "I long to see you in order that I may impart some spiritual gift to you, that you may be established."[598] Paul closes by saying, "[God] is able to establish you according to my

---

597 Tertius was Paul's secretary who was copying down the letter for Paul as he dictated.

598 Romans 1:11

gospel, and the preaching of Jesus Christ."[599] Proclaim Christ, and God's people become established. Proclaim Romans, the gospel as proclaimed in Christ, and God's people become established. Praise be to our Triune God; Father, Son, and Spirit; "to the only wise God, through Jesus Christ, be the glory forever. Amen."[600]

---

599 Romans 16:25
600 Romans 16:27

Study questions

- How does God give us "perseverance and encouragement" (15:4-6)? What are examples in your life?

- What does the "contribution for the poor among the saints in Jerusalem" teach us about the importance of Christian giving (see 15:22-29)?

- How can we use Paul's warnings in 16:17-20 to discern "false teachings" in the church today?

- Who are some of the people who have influenced you on your spiritual journey?

APPENDIX 1

WHY COPY OUT SCRIPTURE?
A PERSONAL TESTIMONY

O HOW I LOVE THY LAW!
IT IS MY MEDITATION ALL THE DAY.

LAST FRIDAY AS I PUT DOWN MY PENCIL AT THE CONCLUSION OF COPYING OUT PSALM 150, I FOUND MYSELF REJOICING IN GOD'S WORD ONCE MORE, IT WAS A MEMORABLE DAY FOR ME BECAUSE IT MARKED THE CONCLUSION OF COPYING OUT THE BIBLE. I HAD PURPOSELY SAVED PSALM 150 FOR MY CONCLUDING PAGE, BECAUSE IT SEEMS SUCH A FITTING CLOSURE TO THE BOOK OF WORSHIP AND THIS PROJECT OF COPYING OUT THE SCRIPTURE HAS DEFINENTLY BEEN A LABOR OF LOVE AND WORSHIP.

THIRTY SOME YEARS AGO, AS A YOUNG COLLEGE STUDENT, I WAS JUST BEGINNING TO DISCOVER THE JOYS OF SERIOUS BIBLE STUDY. I HAD GIVEN MYSELF TO REPEATED READINGS OF THE BOOK OF ROMANS AND IT WAS YIELDING UP SUCH EXCITING TRUTH FROM GOD THAT I WAS ALMOST OVER-WHELMED, I WAS SO EXCITED ABOUT FIRST-HAND PERSONAL INTERACTION WITH ROMANS THAT I DECIDED TO COPY IT OUT BY HAND. AS I DID SO I LEARNED SO MUCH, SAW THINGS I HADN'T SEEN BEFORE, UNDERSTOOD CONNECTIONS BETWEEN VERSES AND JUST GENERALLY FOUND IT A VERY HELPFUL AND BENEFICIAL EXERCISE.

AFTER THAT EXPERIENCE, I TENDED TO MAKE COPYING OUT SCRIPTURE A PART OF MY DEVOTIONAL HABIT. WHEN I TOOK UP ANOTHER BOOK OF THE BIBLE, I WOULD, AFTER READING IT MANY TIMES, MAKE A HAND WRITTEN COPY. THIS SOMEWHAT MECHANICAL DISCIPLINE WOULD SLOW ME DOWN AND GIVE ME TIME TO MULL OVER AND MEDITATE UPON WHAT GOD WAS SAYING.

SOMETIME AFTER EXPERIENCING THE BENEFIT OF THIS SIMPLE EXERCISE, I READ IN DEUTERONOMY WHERE GOD HAD ACTUALLY PRESCRIBED THIS METHOD OF INTERACTION WITH HIS WORD FOR THE KINGS OF ISRAEL. I WAS PLEASANTLY SURPRISED TO READ THAT, "WHEN HE SITS ON THE THRONE OF HIS KINGDOM, HE SHALL WRITE FOR HIMSELF A COPY OF THIS LAW ON A SCROLL," DEUTERONOMY 17:18. GOD WENT ON TO EXPLAIN SOME OF THE BENEFITS OF THIS THAT INCLUDED:

- LEARNING TO FEAR THE LORD

- BECOMING MORE CAREFUL TO OBEY THE LORD

- BEING PROTECTED FROM PRIDE

- KEEPING ONE FROM WANDERING AWAY FROM THE LORD, "TURNING ASIDE.... TO THE RIGHT OR THE LEFT."

READING THIS IN GOD'S WORD (DEUTERONOMY 17:18-20) NOT ONLY CONFIRMED THE VALUE OF THIS EXERCISE THAT I HAD ALREADY BEEN ENJOYING, BUT IT ALSO MOTIVATED ME TO PERHAPS SOMEDAY COMPLETE THE ENTIRE NEW TESTAMENT, YEARS LATER I DID JUST THAT. I STARTED OVER AND USED A CONSISTENT FORMAT AND TRIED TO KEEP MY COPY NEAT ENOUGH TO BE READABLE. WHEN I COMPLETED THE NEW TESTAMENT, I WAS MOTIVATED TO BEGIN THE OLD. I BEGAN IN GENESIS / AND ABOUT FIVE YEARS LATER, ONE WEEK AGO, FINISHED WITH GREAT JOY IN MY HEART AS I PENNED THE CONCLUDING WORDS TO THAT LAST PSALM.

"LET EVERYTHING THAT HAS BREATH PRAISE THE LORD. PRAISE THE LORD!"

I CAN ONLY SAY AMEN! THE JOY IN MY HEART WAS BORN, NOT SO MUCH FROM FINISHING THE PROJECT, BUT BECAUSE OF THE JOY, THE PERSONAL JOY IN THE PROCESS. IN FACT, A CERTAIN MELANCHOLY CAME OVER ME AS THE PROJECT DREW TO A CLOSE. I WAS SAD THAT IT WAS OVER! BUT THAT MORNING I WAS REMINDED THAT I STILL HAVE PLENTY OF PAPER AND THERE IS NOTHING TO STOP ME FROM CONTINUING TO COPY PORTIONS OR ALL OF THE HOLY SCRIPTURES IN THE FUTURE.

THAT MORNING I TURNED TO THE NINETEENTH PSALM AND SPENT THE REMAINDER OF MY DEVOTIONAL TIME PRAISING THE LORD FOR THE PERFECTION, BEAUTY AND VALUE OF HIS WORD. INDEED, "THE LAW OF THE LORD IS PERFECT" AND IT DOES "RESTORE THE SOUL."

GOD HAS GIVEN US A GOLD MINE IN THE HOLY SCRIPTURE. HE PROMISES GREAT BLESSINGS TO HIS CHILDREN WHO ABIDE IN IT. IN FACT, THERE IS NO HABIT MORE CENTRAL TO EXPERIENCING GOD'S BLESSING AND PERSONALLY GETTING TO KNOW HIM THAN SPENDING TIME ON A REGULAR AND CONSISTENT BASIS IN HIS WORD. IF YOU HAVE NEVER TRIED HAND COPYING HIS WORD, WHY NOT GIVE IT A TRY. YOU MAY FIND, AS I HAVE, THAT IT IS A VERY VALUABLE WAY TO "MEDITATE DAY AND NIGHT" AND "DELIGHT IN THE LAW OF THE LORD."

SCOTT GILCHRIST
MAY 2004

"NOW IT SHALL COME ABOUT WHEN HE SITS ON THE THRONE OF HIS KINGDOM, HE SHALL WRITE FOR HIMSELF A COPY OF THIS LAW ON A SCROLL IN THE PRESENCE OF THE LEVITICAL PRIESTS.

AND IT SHALL BE WITH HIM, AND HE SHALL READ IT ALL THE DAYS OF HIS LIFE, THAT HE MAY LEARN TO FEAR THE LORD HIS GOD, BY CAREFULLY OBSERVING ALL THE WORDS OF THIS LAW AND THESE STATUTES,

THAT HIS HEART MAY NOT BE LIFTED UP ABOVE HIS COUNTRYMEN AND THAT HE MAY NOT TURN ASIDE FROM THE COMMANDMENT, TO THE RIGHT OR THE LEFT; IN ORDER THAT HE AND HIS SONS MAY CONTINUE LONG IN HIS KINGDOM IN THE MIDST OF ISRAEL."

DEUTERONOMY 17:18-20

APPENDIX 2
ROMANS PROJECT

Romans Project is a non-profit corporation established to equip pastors to abide in and feed their congregations from God's word. It does that by challenging pastors to read the book of Romans twenty times and write it out by hand. When a pastor completes the challenge, they are given a pocket-sized Mp3 player that contains over one hundred biblical expository messages on the book of Romans by Pastor Scott Gilchrist, senior pastor at SW Bible Church in Beaverton, Oregon. The Mp3 player also contains over 800 expository messages on other books of the Bible. Pastors are encouraged to repeat this method of reading, writing by hand, and listening through God's word being taught, as they continue to grow and walk in truth.

Romans Project was founded by John Corey, a career missionary, who began taking Mp3 players containing biblical expository messages to Liberia in 2005. Corey had been serving as a missionary in Ethiopia and Liberia since 1964. He encouraged a handful of Liberian pastors to read the book of Romans 20 times and copy it into a notebook. Upon completion, each pastor was given the Mp3 player containing expository messages. Within just a few months, 70 pastors had completed the challenge. Corey's life is told in more detail in the book *"Any Ol' Bush Will Do; The Life Story of John Corey"* (2016). Since then, the project has rapidly expanded with thousands of pastors involved and thousands of congregations being impacted by God's Word throughout Africa and, more recently, South Asia.

Anyone interested in learning more about Romans Project or donating to the initiative is encouraged to go to https://www.romansproject.org.